UTTER JUSTICE

UTTER JUSTICE

Verbal Glimpses Into Fifteen Hundred Years Of Our Legal History

Alfred H. Knight

iUniverse, Inc.
New York Bloomington Shanghai

Utter Justice
Verbal Glimpses Into Fifteen Hundred Years Of Our Legal History

Copyright © 2008 by Alfred H. Knight

All rights reserved. No part of this book may be used or reproduced by any means, graphic, electronic, or mechanical, including photocopying, recording, taping or by any information storage retrieval system without the written permission of the publisher except in the case of brief quotations embodied in critical articles and reviews.

iUniverse books may be ordered through booksellers or by contacting:

iUniverse
1663 Liberty Drive
Bloomington, IN 47403
www.iuniverse.com
1-800-Authors (1-800-288-4677)

Because of the dynamic nature of the Internet, any Web addresses or links contained in this book may have changed since publication and may no longer be valid.

The views expressed in this work are solely those of the author and do not necessarily reflect the views of the publisher, and the publisher hereby disclaims any responsibility for them.

ISBN: 978-0-595-47556-8 (pbk)
ISBN: 978-0-595-91825-6 (ebk)

Printed in the United States of America

Contents

PREFACE ix
1. THE PRESUMPTION OF GUILT 1
2. THE SPEEDIEST APPLICATION OF THE RIGHT TO A SPEEDY TRIAL 2
3. THE FIRST CREATION OF THE GRAND JURY 3
4. THE CAPITAL PUNISHMENT DEBATE BEGINS 5
5. MAKING THE PUNISHMENT FIT THE CRIME 7
6. THE WAR BETWEEN CHURCH AND STATE BEGINS IN ERNEST 9
7. THE NEAR-DEATH OF CONSTITUTIONAL LAW 11
8. THE BIRTH OF AN INDEPENDENT JUDICIARY 12
9. THE PAINFUL "RIGHT" TO TRIAL BY JURY 14
10. THE KNOWLEDGEABLE JURY 16
11. HISTORY'S BEST CROSS-EXAMINATION ANSWER 18
12. GUILTY JURIES 19
13. GALLOWS HUMOR 21
14. THE ULTIMATE LEGAL TECHNICALITY 23
15. DOPEY POPE 24
16. "LAWYER-BASHING" AS A TRUE ART FORM 25
17. THE DEPTHS OF JUDICIAL SILLINESS 27
18. THE RULE OF LAW BEGINS TO SPEAK 29
19. THE EARLIEST GOVERNMENT ANTI-SMOKING WARNING ... 30
20. A FRENCH LEGAL TECHNICALITY GIVES BIRTH TO THE FIRST ENGLISH CONSTITUTION 31

21.	THE FIRST FREEDOM OF INFORMATION ACT 33
22.	A FAILED REHEARSAL OF THE AMERICAN REVOLUTION 34
23.	THE WORST JUDGE EVER 35
24.	THE FINAL "PUT-DOWN" OF ENGLISH TYRANNY 37
25.	THE MOST HORRIFYING SLIP OF THE TONGUE BY A WITNESS 39
26.	THE WORST OCCUPATIONAL AND CHILD SAFETY LAW 41
27.	VOLUNTEERING FOR PROSECUTION 42
28.	AN AMERICAN LAWYER DOES HIS JOB 43
29.	THE MOST FATEFUL OMISSION FROM THE DECLARATION OF INDEPENDENCE 45
30.	THE NEAREST MISS ON A MOMENTOUS HISTORICAL PREDICTION 47
31.	THE MOST OVERRATED STATEMENT IN SUPPORT OF FREEDOM OF THE PRESS 48
32.	KING GEORGE "MAKES UP" WITH AMERICA 49
33.	THE MOST ASTOUNDING COURTROOM MIS-IDENTIFICATION OF A CRIMINAL DEFENDANT 50
34.	THE POWER OF PLAGIARISM 52
35.	THE MOST GROSSLY OVERRATED LINE BY A FAMOUS LEGAL ORATOR 55
36.	GREATNESS IN DISGUISE 56
37.	A LAWYER SHRINKS INTO A JUDGE 57
38.	BY THE LIGHT OF THE NON-EXISTENT MOON 59
39.	A MEMORABLE SUPREME COURT ARGUMENT NO ONE REMEMBERS 61
40.	THE SUPREME COURT'S BLOODIEST SELF-INFLICTED WOUND 63
41.	A VERY SMALL VERDICT IN A VERY LARGE CASE 65
42.	LETTING DEFENDANTS OFF ON SPELLING AND GRAMMAR 67

43. A MOST LETHAL CROSS-EXAMINATION 69
44. A TRAGIC CASE OF TESTIMONIAL SUICIDE 73
45. AN UNANSWERABLE FINAL ARGUMENT 76
46. THE MOST TELLING COMMENT ON JUDICIAL TENURE BY A SUPREME COURT JUSTICE 78
47. THE MOST COLORFUL REPUDIATION OF A SUPREME COURT JUSTICE BY THE PRESIDENT WHO APPOINTED HIM 79
48. THE LOUDEST BACKFIRE OF A COURTROOM ARGUMENT 81
49. A CELEBRATED TESTIMONIAL DISTORTION 83
50. THE WORST ADVICE ABOUT A SUPREME COURT APPOINTMENT 84
51. AN ANTI-CLIMACTIC ENDING TO A CELEBRATED CASE 86
52. AN INELEGANT EXPLANATION OF A DECISION BY AN ELOQUENT JUSTICE 88
53. A POETIC DESCRIPTION OF THE MODERN TREND OF JUDICIAL DECISION-MAKING 89
54. ZOOLOGY AS LAW 91
55. A GREAT LIBEL OF A GREAT JUSTICE 93
56. A CREATIVE DEFENSE TO A BRIBERY CHARGE BY A CROOKED JUDGE 95
57. THE MOST DESPISED SUPREME COURT JUSTICE 97
58. AN INSIGHTFUL LITERARY DESCRIPTION OF REAL JURY ATTITUDES 99
59. FEAR SWALLOWS DUE PROCESS 101
60. UNMASKING ROBIN HOOD 104
61. THE BEST USE OF SHAKESPEARE IN A FINAL ARGUMENT 106
62. AN ELOQUENT MOMENT IN THE HISTORY OF CAPITAL PUNISHMENT 108

63. A SMALL TESTIMONIAL FUSE LIGHTS A HUGE POLITICAL EXPLOSION 110
64. A DEPRESSINGLY "REALISTIC" VIEW OF THE AMERICAN TRIAL PROCESS 113
65. AN ILL-ADVISED LITERARY FLOURISH 115
66. GIVE ME LIBERTY OR GIVE ME—SOMETHING 116
67. THE SUPREME COURT'S GREAT PHILOSOPHICAL DIVIDE 118
68. AN ANTIQUATED RULE MEETS ITS LONG OVERDUE FATE 119
69. THE ONLY JUSTICE KNOWN TO HAVE DISSENTED FROM HIS OWN MAJORITY OPINION 121
70. HUGO IN WONDERLAND 123
71. A MOMENTOUS APOLOGY 124
72. HOPPING ABOARD PRESIDENT KENNEDY'S HEARSE 127
73. AN HISTORIC LOW IN PSYCHIATRIC TESTIMONY 129
74. THE MOST QUOTED JUDICIAL STATEMENT SINCE THE RETIREMENT OF OLIVER WENDELL HOLMES 131
75. THE WORD LOS ANGELES MUNICIPAL COURT DEFENSE LAWYERS MOST DREADED TO HEAR 133
76. THE QUIET BEGINNING OF THE DESTRUCTION OF A PRESIDENCY 137
77. AN HISTORIC DOUBLE ENTENDRE 139
78. A CRUEL AND UNUSUAL DECISION 140
79. THE STRANGEST RIGHT OF PRIVACY DECISION OF ALL TIME 142
80. DRUNKEN JUSTICE 144
81. DEFENDING SOCIETY AGAINST CONFESSIONS 146
82. THE LAW BECOMES SENILE IN ITS OLD AGE 148
83. CAPITAL PUNISHMENT TURNS WACKY 150
84. THE SUPREME COURT'S SECOND WORST DECISION 153

PREFACE

Andrew Jackson once said of a Supreme Court decision: "The Court have made their decree, now let them enforce it." The old warhorse had a point, but not a very strong one. It is true that law consists of words which in themselves are not coercive, but they are obeyed out of a nearly universal sense of obligation, which is the reflex of a people who are used to living by the rule of law. The words of justices and judges are not guaranteed to have real world effects unless they are enforced at the point of guns and bayonets, but for well over a thousand years words unaccompanied by force have usually sufficed.

This book is a compilation of legal and law-related statements that have defined and characterized our legal system over the centuries. But the reader will quickly recognize that it is not a textbook in disguise. The quotations, and the actions and ideas they present and represent were selected by purely personal criteria: the author found them fascinating, important, or revealing. They range from history-changing statements (Henry II's "will no one rid me of this turbulent priest!") to purely mythological encounters (Lincoln's cross-examination of "Sovine" about the phase the moon was in when a murder took place) to royal chit-chat (a devastating remark a high-born lady made to the fugitive King James II which can be viewed as the final word on English royal tyranny) to an apology made in a casual encounter on an American street that symbolized the healing of a terrible cultural wound. The hope is to convey, not a rigid history, but a random flavor of how the law has been shaped by calculated, casual, powerful, and even silly words, uttered for the ages or merely for the moment.

This disparate verbal collection tells us that our legal system is not like a carefully sculptured statue, but like a human being, is composed of all that it has known and done and said.

1.

THE PRESUMPTION OF GUILT

> "If any far coming man or a stranger journey through a wood out of the highway, and neither shout nor blow his horn, he is to be held for a thief ... to be slain."
>
> Seventh Century Saxon law.

This ancient law confers an extraordinary right of self-defense—an approaching stranger can be summarily killed if he does not announce his honest intentions. We think of David Berkowitz who shot three approaching teenagers on a New York subway and claimed self-defense because he thought they meant him harm. He was impulsively acting in accordance with ancient Saxon law, exercising a preemptive right of execution on the <u>assumption</u> that the strangers were <u>probably</u> a threat.

Our own legal system, of course, presumes innocence. The spirit of that presumption pervades every aspect of criminal process, from arrest, to interrogation, to trial, until conviction. At least in theory, we treat criminal suspects with fairness and dignity—as "one of us"—until guilt is fairly proven.

The ancient Saxons, who lived every day in peril of their lives and property, could not afford this luxury. They would have considered a presumption of innocence a form of insanity. Nothing so clearly marks the success of society's journey from their age to ours as the transformation of a presumption of guilt into a presumption of innocence. By the same token, the more our streets and subways come to resemble the paths and highways of the Saxons, the more our laws will come to resemble theirs.

2.

THE SPEEDIEST APPLICATION OF THE RIGHT TO A SPEEDY TRIAL

"If a thief be seized, let him perish by death.... If any thief or robber flee to the King, or to any church and to the bishop, that he have a term of nine days. And if he flee to an ealdorman or to an abbot or to a thegn let him have a term of three days."

Ninth Century Saxon law.

One of our most important constitutional rights is the right to a "speedy trial". It seldom comes into play; prosecutions usually descend on defendants while their counsel are doing their best to catch up with well-prepared prosecutors. Nonetheless, the right is fundamental. Otherwise indicted people might wait endlessly in jail while the government slow-walked them to trial. Maximum sentences might be served in pre-trial detention before the accused ever got to see a courtroom.

As the above quote demonstrates, our Dark Ages ancestors faced no such problems. The one abuse Saxon defendants could not complain about was delay in prosecution. Justice was nothing if not swift. And for the most part justice <u>was</u> nothing—no lawyers, no juries, no evidence—so why <u>should</u> it be delayed?

3.

THE FIRST CREATION OF THE GRAND JURY

> "That a gamut be held in every wapontake; and the twelve thegns go out, and the reeve with them, and swear on the relic that is given them in hand, that they will accuse no innocent man, nor conceal any guilty one."
>
> Decree of English King Ethelred "The Unready", 997.

This looks like the summoning of a grand jury: twelve distinguished citizens are to be gathered together to swear under oath which of their fellow citizens should be accused of crimes. But most legal historians agree that the grand jury was invented in 1166, when Henry II issued his famous Assize of Clarendon:

> "Inquires shall be made in every hundred ... by <u>the twelve most lawful men of the hundred</u>, upon oath that they shall speak the truth, whether in their hundred ... there be any man who is accused or believed to be a robber, murderer, thief, or receiver of robbers, murderers, thieves since the King's accession."

Henry's creation of the grand jury is a large part of the reason he is considered the father of English justice. He supposedly got the idea from the Frankish Inquest, which William the Conqueror brought to England in 1066. William's inquests were groups of English subjects summoned to provide information about such things as title to land and personal property holdings, operating like modern census takers. It is said that Henry originated the idea of using such citizen groups to make criminal accusations.

But Henry's description of his grand jury bears an obvious and suspicious similarity to Ethelred's description of the "gamut of twelve thegns" 169 years earlier. Note in particular the remarkable coincidence that Ethelred's and Henry's grand juries both had twelve members. (Since 1166 the number has fluctuated wildly, from more than one hundred to the present twenty-three).

* * * *

The natural conclusion is that Henry, undetected by history, copied Ethelred's 169 year old procedure. But don't try arguing that with a legal history professor; the origin of the grand jury is too well-established for debate. As Napoleon famously said, "history is a fable agreed upon".

4.

THE CAPITAL PUNISHMENT DEBATE BEGINS

> "And we command that Christian men be not on any account for altogether too little condemned to death; but rather let gentle punishments be decreed for the benefit of all people."
>
> King Canute (1016–1035).

Legalized murder, more popularly known as capital punishment, has been the subject of vigorous disputes and profound doubt for many centuries. These disputes and doubts are 1,000 years old, as Canute's quote clearly demonstrates.

Canute's words helped build his image as an unusually humane ruler. They are like a beacon of light in the midst of a barbarous night. The light dims, however, when we learn through his later pronouncements exactly what he meant by "gentle punishments":

> That [the felon's] hand be cut off, or his feet, or both, according as the deed may be. And if he have wrought yet graver wrong, then let his eyes be put out and his nose and his ears and his upper lip be cut off, or let him be scalped.

Later in the century, William Rufus (1087-1100) broadly reinstated the death penalty, although he, too, opposed it in principle. He reasoned that death by hanging was more humane than death by mortified mutilation—the usual result of Canute's "gentle punishments." Canute has been remembered as by far the more civilized of the two.

Canute's superior reputation in this and other respects was largely a matter of public relations. The official English history was the Anglo-Saxon Chronicle, written by monks. Canute was a generous supporter of the Church, whereas William Rufus was a bitter Church enemy. The monks were as susceptible to bias as modern newspaper reporters. As far as their Chronicle was concerned, "Canute made his name renowned," while William Rufus "was hated by almost all his people and was abhorrent to God." The "gentle" Canute could do not wrong; the "brutal" William Rufus could do no right. And never mind those blinded felons suffering festering, mortal wounds—Canute's <u>intentions</u> were superior.

We should not feel overly superior about the Canute/William Rufus debacle. Our own Supreme Court has made an undelectible hash of capital punishment, outlawing it in 1972, reinstating it in an altered and confusing form in 1976, leaving in the wake of successive opinions a jumble of rules for applying it, based on age, mental competence and the circumstances of the crime, that have made the virtually unthinkable virtually incomprehensible. (*See*, p. 15, *infra*).

5.

MAKING THE PUNISHMENT FIT THE CRIME

> "If a man lay with a woman against her will, he is forthwith condemned to forfeit those members with which he has disported himself."
>
> Law of William the Conqueror, 1085.

Eleventh Century records being what they are, it is not clear whether this surgically precise measure deterred rape among the general population. It can safely be assumed, however, that there were no repeat offenders.

Early English law punished most serious crimes by specialized physical afflictions. There was little choice, since there were no prisons for common people. The authorities couldn't lock criminals up, so they beat them up or cut them up in ways that mirrored their crimes. In King Alfred's time (871–899), subjects convicted of slander had their tongues cut out. Amputation of hands was the common punishment for theft. Those who committed multiple felonies could be subjected to multiple "deaths": in the reign of Edward I, William Wallace was drawn for treason, hanged for robbery and homicide, disemboweled for sacrilege, beheaded as an outlaw, and quartered for "divers depredations".

The colonial Americans were equally adept, if less brutal, at specialized punishments. When a servant was convicted of stealing a pair of breeches in Accomack County, Virginia in 1638, he was sentenced to "sitt in the stocks on the next Sabbath day ... from the beginning of morninge prayer until the end of the Sermon with a pair of breeches about his necke." Women convicted of being "common scolds" were condemned to standing gagged in public, or were "cooled off" by being immersed in a ducking pool. Flogging was common throughout the colonial period, one of its advantages being that the punishment could be adjusted to fit the crime by the number of strokes laid on.

In the 19th Century, physical punishment became politically incorrect and was generally abolished, except, of course, for executions. Flogging was the last of the non-fatal physical punishments to go. It was replaced by prolonged confinement, on the ground that striking criminals was too brutal for an enlightened nation.

Some might argue that the abolition of physical punishment is a cruel sort of kindness. Thirty lashes "well-laid on" may seem a terrible punishment, until compared with a few years in jail. Which would you choose, if you had to make the choice? Exactly.

6.

THE WAR BETWEEN CHURCH AND STATE BEGINS IN ERNEST

"Will no one rid me of this turbulent priest!"

King Henry II, 1170.

This inadvertent blurt had profound long term consequences for the development of constitutional law. Henry's hair-trigger tongue ultimately changed the course of English history. It brought about a crisis in church-state relations which reverberated for centuries, profoundly altering the quality of English justice. The "turbulent priest" was Archbishop Thomas Becket, whose efforts to block the prosecution of clergymen in the King's Court had frustrated Henry beyond the short limits of his temper. Henry's immortal blurt was merely a venting of anger during a banquet, but four excessively stupid knights took him at his word. They made Becket England's greatest martyr, murdering him while at prayers before Henry could head them off.

The power of Becket's position increased immensely with his death—Henry could not win an argument with an incipient saint. Within a decade the doctrine of "Benefit of Clergy" was in full force, which meant that every clergyman—and eventually, every citizen who could read—was given immunity from criminal punishment in the King's Court, while illiterate people perished for minor crimes. It was an amazingly unfair process, which maimed English justice for over 600 years.

The injustice of Benefit of Clergy does not really strike home until the comparative plight of illiterate prisoners is considered. The tale is told in the records of the Devenshire criminal court for the year 1598. Five men were convicted of sheep stealing. John Chapan could not read, and was sentenced to death. Gregory Tolman could not read either, but had the luck or influence to have the sheep he stole valued by the jury at less than a shilling, making his crime a misdemeanor. He was flogged and set free. Steven Juall, Andrew Penrose and Anthony Scholston could read, and were simply set free. Comparatively speaking, the "soft", inconsistent sentencing of modern America are models of stern consistency.

* * * *

It is said that Genghis Khan destroyed the flourishing Persian civilization, burning its cities to the ground and diverting rivers to cover their ashes, because of rage over the decapitation (or by some accounts the de-bearding) of one of his couriers. If so, Henry's blurt is only the second costliest temper tantrum of the Middle Ages.

7.

THE NEAR-DEATH OF CONSTITUTIONAL LAW

"[B]y such violence was John forced to accept an agreement that was shameful, illegal and unjust, impairing his royal rights and dignity. Therefore, we utterly reject and condemn this settlement, ordering under threat of excommunication that the King should not dare to observe it nor the barons require it to be observed, and we declare the Charter, with all undertakings arising from it, to be null and void forever."

Bull issued by Pope Innocent III, August 24, 1215.

Almost before the wax had hardened on Magna Charta, the perfidious King John abandoned the oath he had taken to uphold it. He appealed to Rome to be released from it, and the Pope was only too glad to oblige. John went to war against the barons who sought to enforce the Charter, and very nearly prevailed. Magna Charta might, indeed, have become "null and void" before it had time to take root if John had not died in October, 1216, from eating unripe peaches.

Our constitutional rights and freedoms have continued to have close calls since 1215. It is said that Parliament barely passed the great Habeas Corpus Act of 1679, and then only because of a joke—the clerk supposedly multiplied one member's vote by 10 because he was enormously fat. The American constitutional convention of 1787 rejected a Bill of Rights by a vote of 10 states to none; Congress grudgingly adopted one in 1791 only because of strong popular insistence. Today, constitutional rights are widely considered a nuisance, and, like modern Innocent IIIs, many Americans rail against judges who enforce them. If, having escaped infanticide our freedoms die in middle age, we will have no Pope to blame. If and when we meet our freedoms' final enemy, he will be us.

8.

THE BIRTH OF AN INDEPENDENT JUDICIARY

"Common pleas shall not follow our Court, but shall be held in some fixed place."

Magna Charta, Chapter XVII, 1215.

This seldom-noticed provision of Magna Charta was monumentally important, both to contemporary Englishmen and to future generations. It was at least as important in its practical effect as the more famous chapters of the Charter. In it, John promised that his Court of Common Pleas would in the future stand still so that the people could find it.

Early English government was highly personal and highly mobile. Royal justice was administered by the King himself, or by his appointed representatives and, in all cases, the King claimed the right of final decision. The problem was that kings did not sit in marble palaces waiting for plaintiffs to come to them. They were constantly on the move, hunting, fighting, and collecting revenue from their far-flung estates in England and on the continent. John's father and predecessor Henry II had a fine lawyer's eye and mind, and dispensed a superior brand of justice, but a claimant might run himself to death and spend himself into bankruptcy chasing the energetic monarch in search of it.

A flagrant case in point was that of Richard d'Anesty (1158–1163). In his efforts to establish his right to his deceased uncle William's lands, d'Anesty was forced to chase the King's justice all over England and Normandy.

He pursued Henry to Normandy, Salisbury, South Hampton, Ongar, North Hampton, back to South Hampton, and then to Winchester, Lambeth, Maidstone, back to Lambeth, back to Normandy, then to Canterbury, Aviniarium, Mort Lake, back to Canterbury, then to London, to Stafford, once again to Canterbury, then to Wingham, Rome, back to Winchester, then to Oxford, Lincoln, once again to Winchester, then to Rumsey, back to Rome, back to London, then to Windsor, and finally to Woodstock. It took him five years and cost him enormous sums of money—mostly for traveling expenses—borrowed at interest rates of eighty-six and two-thirds percent (86 2/3%) per annum, before he finally obtained judgment.

The barons of Runnymede had this and similar horror stories in mind when they insisted that Article XVII be included in Magna Charta. The measure did not eliminate outrageously expensive justice (lawyer's fees would soon replace travel expenses in that regard) but it did for a time make justice more efficient and less exhausting.

It had a larger effect. When the royal courts became fixed in place and separate from the King, they began to grow as independent institutions of government. With the King no longer looking over their shoulders, the judges began to regard themselves, and to be regarded, as authorities unto themselves. Four centuries later, Chief Justice Coke told an astonished King James I that the King was subject to the law declared by the courts. He could never have made that earthshaking statement if the King's justices had remained part of his household.

The roots of the modern independent judiciary, and all of its works, can be traced to Article XVII of Magna Charta. As in other cases, the barons of Runnymede wrought much greater than they knew.

9.

THE PAINFUL "RIGHT" TO TRIAL BY JURY

> "If notorious felons and which openly be of evil name will not put themselves [to trial by jury] they shall have strong and hard imprisonment, as they which refuse to stand to the common law of the land."

Statute of Westminster, 1275.

When jury trials first replaced ordeals as the method of determining guilt or innocence, they were about as popular as prostate cancer. The ordeals may seem brutal to us, but they gave defendants good chances for acquittal. Suspects were blistered with hot irons or thrown bound into water. If their wounds healed within three days or the suspects sank, they were declared innocent; if the burns festered or the suspects floated, they were declared guilty. The chances of acquittal were about 50/50, and in some eras even better. A jury of neighbors was a much tougher test, particularly since the early juries tended to be corrupt, or biased in favor of the prosecution.

The ordeals disappeared after 1215, when the Church would no longer permit priests to conduct them. Trial juries were at first a makeshift substitute, which arose from the practice of asking the grand (accusing) jury to vote a second time on whether the person they had accused was, in fact, guilty. Understandably, most defendants wanted no part of such a process.

Nor could they, at first, be forced to accept it. In the past, accused felons who refused to submit to the ordeal had been outlawed and put to death; but, perhaps because it was a new procedure, submission to a jury was voluntary. When defendants sensibly declined to subject themselves to the judgment of neighbors who had already expressed a suspicion that they were guilty, the government faced a constitutional crisis.

King Edward I provided a brutal remedy with his statute of Westminster. If felons would not willingly accept England's greatest constitutional gift, they would be physically forced to do so by being clapped into a "hard and strong prison". When mere imprisonment failed to do the trick, the screws were tightened. The accused was "ironed, [forced to] lay on the ground in the prison's worst place, [allowed] a little bread one day, [and] a little water the next". The few who still held out were "laden with iron". That is, metal or rocks were piled upon their chests until they either agreed to jury trial, or died.

Those who felt their ribs collapse into their lungs could never have guessed that the jury would in time become our most cherished procedural right. The process of neighbor judging neighbor would be improved and refined and polished until it was a beacon to the world. In the distant future, people would die to preserve a process they had once died to avoid.

We have the best constitutional system in the world not because we have been wise, but because we have been flexible. The principles contained in our Bill of Rights were not created, they grew. People who insist that we should interpret these rights according to their "original intent" have not read their history. The statute of Westminster would be a good place start.

10.

THE KNOWLEDGEABLE JURY

> "If the greater part of [the jurors] know the facts and the other part do not, judgment shall be according to the opinion of the greater. And if they declare upon their oaths that they know nothing of the facts, <u>let others be called who do know it</u>."

Britton (English Legal Commentator), 1292.

Compare that 13th Century celebration of jury pre-knowledge with our own insistence on juror ignorance:

> An examination of the 2,783 page [jury selection] record shows that 370 prospective jurors, or almost 90% of those examined on the point, <u>entertained some opinion as to guilt</u> ... Two-thirds of the jurors had an opinion that petitioner was guilty and were familiar with the material facts and circumstances involved....
> Petitioner's detention and sentence of death pursuant to the void judgment is in violation of the Constitution of the United States, and he is therefore entitled to be freed therefrom.
>
> United States Supreme Court, 1961.

These two passages graphically illustrate the cultural divide between medieval and modern justice. Medieval jurors came to court, not to be told facts, but to tell the judge what the facts and rumors were, and what the defendant's fate should be. That conclusion was not formed in the courtroom, but out in the "country", where guilt or innocence were "known".

When a medieval defendant "put himself upon the Country" he experienced something closer to a modern election than a modern jury trial. He was judged by what his jurors knew, believed, suspected, conjectured or wanted to believe about his guilt or innocence before they came to court to cast their votes. Jurors who had no pre-existing opinions regarding his case were considered worthless ignoramuses.

We see Britton describing what is to us a jury selection process in reverse. Instead of entrusting the verdict to those who will listen to testimony with objective fairness, it entrusts it to those who have already made up their minds. What the judge is looking for in prospective jurors is the strongest possible pre-existing "bias"; just as our judges look for pre-existing ignorance and indifference.

Justice is, truly, in the eyes of the culture it serves.

11.

HISTORY'S BEST CROSS-EXAMINATION ANSWER

Q: "Do you know if you are in the grace of God?"
A: "If I am not, may God place me there; if I am, may God so keep me. I should be the saddest in all the world, if I knew that I were not in the grace of God."

Joan of Arc, during her trial for heresy in 1431.

With malicious skill, Joan's prosecutor extended to her the Hobson's choice of boasting that she was saved, or confessing that she was not. She declined the choice, with an answer as graceful and adroit as any ever heard in a courtroom. "Was there ever a better answer on cross-examination?" asked legal scholar Charles Curtis. Considering what was at stake (no pun intended), probably not.

Joan's interrogation was an awful ordeal. It was conducted for 15 days by 60 experts in theology who were affiliated with the University of Paris. The interrogators' constant purpose was to trick her into admitting that she was a witch, who had claimed and used supernatural powers. The powerful honesty and simplicity of her answers confounded her learned questioners throughout the interrogation.

In the end, of course, it made no difference how she performed in the staged horror show conducted in the name of the Church. Having answered brilliantly as a witness, she was duly burned at the stake.

God's will be done.

12.

GUILTY JURIES

> "All of the first jury shall be committed to the King's prison, their goods shall be confiscated, their possessions seized into the King's hands, their habitations and houses shall be pulled down, their woodlands shall be felled, their meadows shall be plowed up and they themselves forever thenceforth be esteemed in the eye of the law infamous."
>
> John Fortesque (circa 1464), describing the punishment to be imposed upon juries who returned "false" verdicts.

In the beginning juries could be punished for their verdicts. A jury that returned a questionable verdict could have its decision reviewed by a jury of attaint. If this second jury declared the original verdict "false", the dire punishments enumerated by Fortesque could be imposed upon the jurors who had reached it. Historians have noticed a resistance to the performance of civic duties among the Fifteenth Century English and, especially, a profound dislike of jury duty. Distressing!

The practice of punishing jurors for their verdicts was not, however, as crazy as it seems. Medieval juries were more like witnesses than judges. They decided cases on the basis of whatever information they brought with them to court, not on the basis of evidence presented to them after they got there. When jurors made findings that lacked credibility, therefore, they were in a real sense making false reports. It was not unnatural to treat them as perjurers, and punish them accordingly.

Besides, there was no other remedy for bad trial judgments. A party who unfairly lost his case could not obtain a reversal of the judgment, because there was no system of appeals. Like a modern litigant victimized by perjured testimony, his only remedy was whatever satisfaction he derived from seeing the wrongdoers punished.

Slowly, very slowly, the English legal system got it right. Jurors became (supposedly) objective fact-judgers, who based their verdicts on evidence brought before them, and errors were corrected by appeals. Jurors became as safe from retribution as judges. Jury service was still an inconvenient, often boring and exasperating, public duty, but at least it was no longer a potentially disastrous ordeal.

13.

GALLOWS HUMOR

"Help me up, Lieutenant, and as for my coming down, I shall fend for myself."

Thomas More, upon arriving at the scaffold, 1535.

The infliction of the death penalty in modern America is a horrifying sight. The silently or noisily terrified prisoner is strapped to the device which will kill him, and stares through a glass panel at a small, grim audience of watchers. He is a breathing dead man, waiting to become meat. If offered a chance to say last words, he usually shakes his head in desperate silence. As he dies, the audience has difficulty watching and only the ones most wounded by his crimes feel any satisfaction. At best, it is considered a piece of dreadful, if necessary surgery, and few would ever want to watch it happen twice.

Executions were once viewed quite differently. In their heyday, they were cathartic "butcheries of God," that attracted throngs of enthralled spectators. The executions of prominent men combined elements of state funerals, Hollywood openings and stand-up comedy routines. Witty last words were expected. As Sir Walter Raleigh approached his death, he felt the blade of the axe and, smiling, said, "This is sharp medicine, but it will cure all diseases … " When the executioner told him to face to the East on the block, he replied, "So the heart be right, it is no matter which way the head be laid … Think you I fear the shadow of the axe when I fear not the axe itself?"

The selection of Sir Thomas More's quip as the best of the genre is admittedly arbitrary. None of these pre-prepared statements were very funny, and More's was no funnier than most. It does, however, convey the spirit of such occasions, so alien to our own attitude. More worth remembering are Sir Thomas' literal last words. As he knelt to the block, he summed up the terrible dilemma that had brought him to his death, saying, "I die the King's good servant, but God's first."

Today we conduct our executions in barren secrecy, and devise the least painful ways to kill our most predatory criminals. We kill without pageantry, wit or joy. In doing so, we sense a paradox and our sense is right. We execute the way we do because we no longer fully believe in capital punishment, and not believing makes us guiltier, in a sense, than our ancestors who enthusiastically did "God's butchery".

14.

THE ULTIMATE LEGAL TECHNICALITY

"[B]y the custom of this realm, the jurors of the county where [a murdered] party died of [a] stroke can take no knowledge of the said stroke, being in a foreign county, [whereas] the jurors of the county where the stroke was given cannot take knowledge of the death in another county."

Preface to an English statute, 1548.

In the 16th Century, a man could literally get away with murder. The circumstances had to be just right. It all depended upon two concepts inherited from the early Middle Ages: a grand jury could not return an indictment unless it "knew" the facts of the offense, and a grand jury could not "know" facts that occurred outside its own county. Armed with these rusty weapons any man, with a little luck or good planning, could commit the perfect murder. He need only strike his victim a mortal blow, or give him a fatal dose of poison, and then transport him across a county line before he died. A delicate task, but worth the effort—for if he was successful, he could elude the criminal justice system forever. The jury in County B, where the victim died, could not "know" the cause of his death, because the blow or poison was administered in County A, and the jury in County A could not "know" that the blow or poison had killed him, because the death occurred in County B. Each grand jury was legally blinded to half of the crime, and therefore, neither could accuse the perpetrator of the whole crime.

Interesting game, murder.

15.

DOPEY POPE

> "What a valiant woman she is. It is a pity that Elizabeth and I cannot marry: our children would have ruled the world."
>
> Pope Sixtus, on learning that Queen Elizabeth's Protestant government had executed Mary Queen of Scots, a Catholic, 1587.

This amazing statement is a towering example of the corruption of the 16th Century Catholic Church. Apart from its shocking moral implications, it is the height—or depth—of political cynicism. Queen Elizabeth, whom Pope Sixtus so gallantly praised, was the sworn enemy of Catholicism, whereas Mary Queen of Scots, whose death at Elizabeth's hands he seemed to celebrate, was a Catholic martyr.

Mary had entered England in 1569, seeking sanctuary from her Scottish foes. Fearing Mary as a rival for her throne, Elizabeth kept her imprisoned for 17 years, finally beheading her in 1587. During her imprisonment, Mary was a magnet for Catholic plotters seeking to overthrow Elizabeth. This plotting was encouraged by a Papal decree in 1570, which excommunicated Elizabeth and prohibited her Catholic subjects from obeying her. Elizabeth's government finally decided that, however innocent Mary might personally be, her very existence posed an unacceptable threat, and so they killed her. In a very real sense, the excommunication of Elizabeth by Pope Sixtus' predecessor in office was a contributing cause of Mary's execution—which makes the Pope's apparent approval of Mary's death particularly obscene.

No wonder Martin Luther rebelled.

16.

"LAWYER-BASHING" AS A TRUE ART FORM

"First thing we do, let's kill all the lawyers."

William Shakespeare, Henry VI, part II, (circa 1597).

This line adorns contemporary t-shirts. It is popular because it expresses a common sentiment with simplicity and force. "Let's stop complaining about lawyers—let's just up and <u>kill</u> them. <u>All</u> of them." People who do not know another line of Shakespeare, except "to be or not to be", know and treasure this one.

When the line is read in context, however, it is clearly not a simple case of lawyer-bashing. The homicidal suggestion is made by Dick the Butcher, who is standing in a crowd being harangued by the rebel Jack Cade. Dick quietly mocks everything Cade says about the society he will establish when he overthrows the King. Cade promises, among other things, to make it a felony to drink a small beer, and says he will provide financial support for the entire population, thereby absolving them from the need to work. At this point Dick makes the facetious suggestion that the first order of business should be to "Kill all the lawyers", and Cade readily accepts the suggestion. Then a cleric is brought before him, "accused" of being able to read. "Monstrous", mutters Cade. When the cleric "confesses" that he can write his own name, Cade orders him "hung with his pen-and-ink horn around his neck."

Some lawyers who have read the play are flattered by the "kill the lawyers" line. They believe that Shakespeare is casting the legal profession in the role of civilization's guardian—the outlaw Cade realizes that he cannot overturn civilized society unless he exterminates lawyers, along with literacy.

Maybe so, but the line may actually imply the less positive viewpoint about the place of lawyers in society that the t-shirts express. According to legal philosopher Rosco Pound, it reflects the universal urge "to administer justice without lawyers" which, he says, is "a feature of all utopias, a feature of all revolutions from Jack Cade's rebellion, to the French Revolution, to the Russian revolution." In the century before Shakespeare wrote, Thomas More (himself a lawyer) wrote of a "Utopia" from which lawyers were excluded, on the ground that they are "a sort of people whose practice it is to disguise things". In the century after he wrote, American colonists were attempting to create a superior society in a pristine land, by barring lawyers from courtrooms and prohibiting the payment of legal fees.

But the abolition of lawyers always turns out to be futile and short-lived. In law, as in the rest of life, it is an advantage to know what one is doing, and professionalism inevitably claims its place. As disputes become more sophisticated with the evolution of society, people learn that "he who represents himself has a fool for a lawyer," and eventually, only poor fools do so. The rich ones employ competent counsel.

In a perfect world, lawyers might be expendable, but in the real world a hard truth always emerges; as long as there are fights there will be professional fighters.

17.

THE DEPTHS OF JUDICIAL SILLINESS

"Death is but an inference here."

Court of the King's Bench, in *Holt v. Astrigg*, (1607).

Among the many questionable court decisions made throughout the centuries, a few stand out as truly bad. Some of them are products of simple stupidity. The worst, however, are deliberate. When a court makes a ruling that seems to make no sense at all, you can be fairly certain there is a hidden agenda. The judge wants to reach a given result, and gets there by any means he can. Logic, rationality and fairness are not permitted to stand in the way.

In the early 1600's, there was a rash of terrible decisions in English slander cases. It was as though the courts were flaunting their power by showing that they did not have to pay any attention at all to common sense.

One man filed a complaint claiming that the defendant had called him "as errant a thief as there is in all England". The court dismissed the complaint on the ground that the plaintiff had failed to prove that there were any thieves in England. For all the court knew, the plaintiff might be "as errant as any" and not be a thief at all.

Another suit claimed that the defendant, a married woman, had falsely accused the plaintiff of stealing her turkeys. Sorry, said the court, the accusation is "legally impossible" and therefore not slanderous. A married woman can't own property, so the turkeys could not have been "hers". The suit must fail.

A beer brewer and tavern owner named Dickes sued Fenne, a customer, for saying: "I will feed my mare a peck of malt, and she shall pisse as good beare as Dickes doth brew." This accusation was also held to be "impossible"—a mare, after all, can't actually "pisse beare". Complaint dismissed.

These judges had a hidden agenda. The 17th Century English were a contentious lot and loved to file slander actions. Slander litigation became such a popular sport that lawyers compiled encyclopedias of words that courts had held actionable, for use in "running" cases. The courts were not interested in spending their valuable time refereeing vulgar insult contests and resolved to do as little of it as possible. They devised the so-called "innocent construction rule", which simply meant that they would dismiss slander complaints for any good, bad or ridiculous reason that occurred to them.

The worst of these decisions—and perhaps the worst decision in Anglo-American history—was *Holt v. Astrigg*. Like many slander actions of the time, it had its origin in a pub. In a half-drunk state, the defendant Astrigg had informed a group of tavern "regulars" that Lord Holt had murdered his servant. The precise accusation, as stated in Holt's slander complaint, was that: "Lord Holt hath taken an axe and cleaved his servant over the head, cutting it in twain, so that the one half lay on one shoulder, and the other half on the other shoulder."

Astrigg's counsel moved for dismissal of the complaint on the ground that Astrigg had not accused Lord Holt of murder in clear and unmistakable terms. Amazingly the court agreed, and dismissed the complaint. "Death is but an inference here", the judges solemnly explained. "Notwithstanding such wounding, the party may yet be living, and it is then but trespass ... Slander ought to be direct."

The court really said that. It is a published opinion. You could look it up.

18.

THE RULE OF LAW BEGINS TO SPEAK

"The King is under God and the law."

Chief Justice Edward Coke to James I, 1608.

Popular myth says that the rule of law had its origin in Magna Charta, enacted in 1215. The myth is approximately four hundred years wrong. The dominant place of law in English society was gradually achieved over many centuries by an evolutionary process, and began to truly manifest itself in 1608 when a brave judge had an historic confrontation with his King.

It is an inspiring tableau: Chief Justice Edward Coke looking the tyrant King James I bravely in the eye, and telling him that even he must obey the English law. Less inspiring, but also fascinating, is the seldom-told aftermath of this scene, in which Coke made the shortest descent from glory on record. It is recorded that: "His Majestae ... looking and speaking fiercely with bended fist offered to strike him, which the Lord Coke perceiving, fell flatt on all fower." Coke's pratfall does not demonstrate that he was a coward, or that he has received too much credit for facing up to the King. It does suggest, however, that if the great moments in history had received adequate press coverage, there would be fewer of them.

James of course prevailed in this schoolyard confrontation, but history was on Coke's side. Two years later, in Dr. Bonham's case, Coke would invent the doctrine of judicial review, which empowers courts to declare legislative acts and executive decrees invalid. As a member of Parliament in later years he would author the Petition of Right, the first true written constitution in English history. These were the foundation stones for the great constitutional democracies that would come to be in England and America in future centuries. Meanwhile, James' brand of royal absolutism was painfully curtailed with the execution of his son Charles I in 1649, and was ended for good with the Glorious Revolution of 1689, when William and Mary took the English throne. It all started with James' clenched fist—the gesture of a man who did not understand that history was passing him by.

19.

THE EARLIEST GOVERNMENT ANTI-SMOKING WARNING

"A custom loathsome to the eye, hateful to the nose, harmful to the brain, dangerous to the lungs, and in the black, stinking fume thereof, nearest resembling the horrible Stygian smoke of the Pit that is bottomless."

James I, 1619.

King James despised the New World vice of tobacco smoking and denounced it with considerable verbal flair. Like most tyrants, he was egotistically selective in his likes and dislikes. A hearty imbiber of alcoholic beverages, it did not occur to him that drunkenness could be as dangerous to health and as obnoxious to companions as smoking. He was, after all, the King, and the King did not have to be consistent in his appetites.

The vices of smoking and drinking have, of course, been the subject of double standards in the 20th Century, as well. In the Prohibition Era, the sale of alcohol was a crime and smoking a social grace. Today, attitudes have been reversed to reflect James' love of liquor and loathing of tobacco.

Strong though James' anti-smoking views were, however, government regulation of the tobacco trade would never have entered his mind. Seventeenth Century English law was brutal and oppressive, controlling speech and conduct in ways we would find intolerable. But no 17th Century king ever launched the ultimate invasion of individual conduct that is a hallmark of our political culture—forced protection of citizens from themselves. James' condemnation of tobacco was vitriolic, but he did his subjects the courtesy of letting them smoke, sicken and die on their own. He imposed the Star Chamber on the people, but he spared them the FDA.

20.

A FRENCH LEGAL TECHNICALITY GIVES BIRTH TO THE FIRST ENGLISH CONSTITUTION

"*Soit droit fait comme il est desire.*"

King Charles' reply to Parliament's Petition of Right. (1628).

The first modern constitution, called the Petition of Right, came into being in 1628. The process of creating it began when King Charles' government imprisoned five knights without any hearing or explanation. Their lawyers contended that the government must state the reasons for their imprisonment so that the judges could either bail them or send them to prison on specific charges. When the case was argued, counsel for the prisoners were supported by "shouting and clapping" from the audience, but of course they lost.

The right of *habeas corpus*—that no one can be imprisoned unless specific charges are brought against him—was vigorously asserted in Parliament, several of whose members had been arbitrarily imprisoned for resisting King Charles' arbitrary rule. Their leader Edward Coke argued that Chapter 39 of Magna Charta, which prevented imprisonment except by "the law of the land", guaranteed that right.

The House of Commons adopted this principle and enlarged on it, stating that no free man could be imprisoned without cause, that prisoners brought to court must either be bailed or freed, and that "no tax taillages, loans or benevolences" were to be levied against citizens without the consent of Parliament.

King Charles did not accept Parliament's resolution as law, but he promised to be "fair". He replied that he would maintain his subjects in the "just freedom of their person and the safety of their estates.... You shall find as much security in His Majesty's royal word and promise as in the strength of any law ye can make. And therefore His Majesty desires that no doubt or mistrust may possess any man, but that ye will all proceed unanimously to his business."

Recognizing the vacuousness of this unenforceable royal promise, Commons replied by drawing up a statute, a sort of mini-constitution intended to be <u>binding</u> on the King. It prohibited taxation without Parliamentary consent, imprisonment without cause given, billeting of soldiers without private consent and stated that free men "returned upon a *habeas corpus* ought to be delivered or bailed".

The King responded by explicitly asking the House to "let him know whether they would rest upon his royal word and promise". Coke courageously responded in a thundering Parliamentary speech, informing his colleagues that "sovereign power is no Parliamentary word. Take heed what we yield unto!" he bellowed. "Magna Charta is such a fellow that he will have no sovereign." He declared that the Parliamentary declaration by itself meant nothing, that it was not law unless the King consented to it in the traditional French words, "*soit droit fait comme il est desire*—let right be done as it is desired".

The King replied that "the King willeth that right be done according to the laws and customs of the realm and that the statutes be put in due execution; that his subjects may have no cause to complain of any wrong or oppressions, contrary to their just right and liberty; to the preservation whereof, he holds himself in conscience as well obliged, as of his prerogative". His soothing speech notably omitted the magic phrase "*soit droit fait*—let right be done". The King had legally conceded nothing.

The House of Lords then joined the Commons in its efforts. A joint committee was dispatched to ask His Majesty for a clear and satisfactory answer to Parliament's petition to enact the new law. In response a royal clerk was sent to Parliament, who stated that Charles was willing to "please" it, "as well in words as in substance". The petition was to be read again and the clerk would give the King's answer. The petition was read and the clerk stepped forward. "*Soit droit fait comme il est desire*", he read.

The modern era of Anglo-American constitutional law had been launched, ironically by the utterance of an ancient French technicality. The French government itself would remain strictly autocratic for more than a century and a half.

21.

THE FIRST FREEDOM OF INFORMATION ACT

"Every inhabitant of the Country shall have free libertie to search and veewe any Rules, Records or Requests of any Court or office except the Council. And to have a transcript or exemplification thereof written, examined and signed by the hand of the officer, paying the appointed fees thereof."

Massachusetts Bodie of Liberties, 1641.

One of the rare defects of our Constitution is its failure to provide a right of access to government information. It is an odd omission, since the Framers certainly understood the importance of such a right. James Madison said that a democracy without knowledge of the operations of its government "was a prelude to a tragedy or a farce". But it was not until 1967, when the Freedom of Information Act was passed by Congress, that American citizens were given the right to know what its government was doing.

Massachusetts was, in this sense, 326 years ahead of its time. Western civilization's first comprehensive constitution—the Bodie of Liberties of 1641—gave all citizens the right to see and copy government documents (the notable exception being "the proceedings of the Council"). This remarkable first American Constitution outdid the Federal Constitution in a number of other respects, providing special legal protection for women, slaves, and even animals. In certain ways, we have not caught up with it yet.

22.

A FAILED REHEARSAL OF THE AMERICAN REVOLUTION

> "But, I thank God, there are no free schools nor printing, and I hope we shall not have these for a hundred years; for learning has brought disobedience and heresy, and sects into the world, and printing has divulged them, and libels against the best government. God keep us from both."
>
> Governor William Berkeley of Virginia, 1671.

The Governor's syntax seems a bit shaky in spots; perhaps he could have done with a little free schooling himself. Notwithstanding his devotion to ignorance, the Virginia colony he governed in time developed an amazing concentration of intellectual talent, becoming a hotbed of "disobedience and heresy", which led to Western civilization's first great revolution in 1776. It's too bad the old bastard didn't have the gift of prophecy, so that he could have suffered from the vision.

Actually, he got a strong foretaste of the great events to come. He was the villain in a rehearsal of the American Revolution, called Bacon's Rebellion. Nathaniel Bacon was the immigrant son of aristocratic English parents, who led a revolt against Berkeley's elitist government in the 1670's.

The mini-revolution was quickly crushed but it became the subject of song and story, and helped inspire the successful American Revolution a century later. With some justice, Bacon has been called the 17th Century forerunner of Thomas Jefferson, and Berkeley has been cast as a low-rent George III.

Like the leaders of 1776, Bacon was highly educated, having graduated from England's Cambridge University. Like them, he possessed the weapon tyrants most fear—an informed vision of something better. Berkeley's words, on the other hand, were the reflex of a near-sighted bully, who fears being blinded by a painful source of light. Unfortunately, however, the military balance of power doomed Bacon's brave uprising. Like so many of history's great revolutions ours required a bloody rehearsal; brave people had to fail before their better empowered successors could succeed.

23.

THE WORST JUDGE EVER

"Oh, how hard the truth is to come out of a lying Presbyterian knave!"

Judge George Jeffries, presiding in the treason trial of Lady Alice Lisle, 1685.

George Jeffries has a well-earned reputation as the fiercest judge in Anglo-American history. Like 17th Century English ship captains, their judicial counterparts had total power over their domains. As an abuser of that power Jeffries was the Captain Bligh of the English legal system.

The great historian T.B. MacCauley painted Jeffries as the Devil incarnate. MacCauley refers to the "mass of infamy with which the memory of the wicked judge has been loaded", and says that "his depravity has passed into proverb". His physical description of Jeffries would make any defendant sick with fear:

> The glare of his eyes had a fascination for the unhappy victim on whom they were fixed. Yet his brow and his eye were said to be less terrible than the lines of his mouth. His yell of fury, as said by one who had heard it, sounded like the thunder of the judgment day.

One of Jeffries' specialties was terrorizing witnesses, a particularly evil example of which occurred in the treason trial of Lady Alice Lisle. The charge itself was a travesty. Out of compassion, Lady Alice had sheltered and nursed some wounded men who were rebels to the Crown. This was constructive treason under the unjust laws of the time and made her subject to the death penalty. Realizing that the jury's natural sympathy for the gentle, elderly defendant created a strong probability that his prey would escape him, Jeffries went to work with a vengeance. He especially went to work on a witness named Dunne, whose doom was sealed by his sympathy for the defendant.

Jeffries berated and intimidated Dunne, who at last grew silent from terror. The inflamed judge then launched into a furious tirade, literally driving Dunne from the witness stand. "Oh, how hard the truth is to come out of a lying Presbyterian knave!", he bellowed. "Was there ever such a villain on the face of the earth? Doest thou believe there is a God? Doest thou believe in hell fire?" He seemed to subside, but then flared up again. "Of all the witnesses I have met" he exclaimed, "I never saw thy fellow.... What a generation of vipers we do live among! ... Was there ever such an impudent rascal?" Jeffries gestured to the bailiff, saying, "Hold the candle to him that we may see his brazen face!" He then turned to the prosecutors and shouted, "You, gentlemen that are counsel for the Crown, see that an information for perjury be prepared against this fellow!"

The jury got the message. When the verdict of guilty was returned, Jeffries ordered that Lady Lisle be burned that afternoon. Royal mercy intervened, however, and her sentence was "reduced" to beheading in five days.

Four years later, the Revolution of 1689 brought William and Mary to the English throne and better justice to the English courts. The coliseum-like atmosphere of the old trials was replaced by the theater-like atmosphere of the new. The right to subpoena favorable witnesses and confront unfavorable ones was granted, and defense counsel were allowed in the more serious cases. Most importantly, judges were expected to conduct themselves with at least the pretense of fairness and civility. This new expectation, subtle and un-legislated, was the most important factor in civilizing English justice. Fortunately, George Jeffries was not only the worst, he was one of the last, of a vicious, destructive breed.

24.

THE FINAL "PUT-DOWN" OF ENGLISH TYRANNY

"Madam, your countrymen have run away."
"Your Majesty seems to have won the race."

Exchange between James II and Lady Tyrconnel (1689).

1689 marked the end of one of the bloodiest eras in English legal history. Throughout the century, religious conflict had produced horrendously unfair prosecutions and horrendously cruel punishments. James I (1603-25) and Charles I (1625-48) converted the beneficent Star Chamber into a brutal instrument of royal policy. "The days of the Commonwealth" (1648-60) were, in the laconic words of W.H. Maitland, "the worst ones for witches." During that 13 year period, the Puritans—who were themselves emerging from an era of vicious persecution—burned and hanged at least 109 persons for witchcraft. The reign of Charles II (1660-85) featured the Popish plot trials, in which blatant perjury combined with popular hatred of Catholics to cause judicial murder of scores of innocent people.

The short reign of James II (1685-88) was the worst of all. A secret Catholic, who came out of the closet when made King, James used the English legal system as a scourge to flail rebellious Puritans into submission. He authorized the Bloody Assizes, during which 320 Puritan peasants were hanged, 841 were transported to the West Indies under conditions so dreadful that a quarter of them died on the way, and brutal whippings were prescribed for minor crimes.

James was the last of England's tyrant kings. In December, 1688, he hurled the Great Seal of England into the Thames, and fled the country, which was rising against him. His last gasp came in July of 1689. Allied with Irish rebels and still hoping for a restoration, he witnessed his forces being routed and scattered by English troops. He withdrew from the vicinity of the battle to more gentile surroundings, where he railed against his allies for their lack of fortitude. Having a sharp wit, and nothing to fear from the ruined King, his hostess Lady Tyrconnel, an Irish noblewoman, made her cheeky response to his complaint quoted above. Her gentle insolence was a perfect reflection of the new, more populist age at hand. There could have been no more eloquent way to usher out the bad old times, and welcome in the better ones to come.

25.

THE MOST HORRIFYING SLIP OF THE TONGUE BY A WITNESS

"Hollowed be Thy name."

Salem witch trials, 1692.

In 1692, a plague of the spirit struck the American town of Salem, Massachusetts like an unnatural disaster. It began in the spring with a pyramiding series of witchcraft accusations, made mostly by hysterical children. By August, eighteen innocent people had been hanged and another had been pressed to death with stones for refusing to admit his compact with the Devil. Due process of law was nowhere to be seen. The trials began by parading the children and other accusers before the Tribunal. Convicted witches were then brought in to confirm that the accused was a sister or brother in damnation. The judges accepted the sworn testimony of these confessed enemies of God with no apparent sense of irony. Next came the disgusting search for bodily imperfections supposedly indicating satanic contact, popularly called "witch marks". Prisoners were stripped and minutely examined by juries of their own sex. If any mole, wart or other "strange" mark was found, it was punctured with a pin to determine whether the Devil had extracted the feeling from it. If the prisoner exhibited no pain, she or he was in great trouble.

Much of the accusatory testimony was factually commonplace, and deadly for that very reason. A grey cat had jumped into the lap of an accused. No problem there, except the witness "knew" that it was the Devil hiding in a cat's body. An accused man had demonstrated great strength by holding his heavy rifle in one hand at arm's length, and carrying a barrel of molasses by inserting his fingers into the bung hole. In most times and places, he would have been admired for his strength. In the psychotic swamp of Salem, he was condemned for having made a pact with the Devil, and put to death.

In some ways, the most frightening procedures were the verbal tests. Prisoners were required to repeat the Lord's prayer, and errors—particularly if subject to an evil interpretation—were considered incriminating. One prisoner made the ghastly mistake of saying "hollowed be Thy name", instead of "hallowed by Thy name". This slip of the tongue "was counted as a depraving of the words [to signify] a curse rather than a prayer" and the defendant was sent to the hangman. It would be hard to find a more grotesque miscarriage of justice anywhere in history.[1]

Those who found themselves facing sudden death on such trivial grounds must have had an impulse to wake themselves from the nightmare. It still seems like a nightmare—the age that produced John Locke and Isaac Newton hanging old women because they were too frightened to give flawless recitations of a prayer. The Reverend Cotton Mather was in many ways a rational, even scientific-minded leader—he was, for example, a strong advocate of vaccination at a time when many people ignorantly opposed it. Yet, he was at the forefront of the Salem Holocaust and his father Increase Mather wrote a learned treatise explaining how the Devil can assume the shape of even a pious person. He was the president of Harvard College at the time.

The ultimate horror of the witch hunts was that they wore the mask of civilization so well. That may be the deepest reason we have never lost our fear of them, and never should.

---

[1] Actually the Salem trials themselves furnished a comparable example. Another prisoner who thought that she had recited perfectly was given the horrifying news that she had said deliver us from *all* evil instead of deliver us from evil . Her judges interpreted this to mean that she sought relief from every mortal threat, including the one she is now justly under . She, too, was ordered into eternity.

26.

THE WORST OCCUPATIONAL AND CHILD SAFETY LAW

"If a master gives correction to his servant it ought to be with the proper instrument, as a cudgel, etc. And then if by accident a blow gives death this would be but manslaughter. The same law of a school master. But a sword is not a proper instrument for correction."

Justice John Holt, *Rex v. Keite* (1697).

This is not the statement of a judicial sadist. Holt was considered one of the most compassionate judges of his generation and was simply stating the law as he found it. What he found was definitely not OSHA.

27.

VOLUNTEERING FOR PROSECUTION

> "The defendant hath falsely and maliciously accused the plaintiff of being an 'highway man'."
>
> The Complaint in *Johnson v. Browning*, 6 Mod. Rep. 217 (1705).

The defendant Browning had, indeed, made the accusation against the plaintiff Johnson, <u>and</u> he was prepared to prove it. He responded to Johnson's complaint for defamation by filing a plea of "justification", stating that the charge was true. This created a jury issue as to whether Johnson was, in fact, a "highway man". Browning proved to the satisfaction of the jury that Johnson was, successfully defending the case. Before Johnson could leave the courtroom, he was arrested, jailed, indicted and prosecuted on a charge of highway robbery, based upon the testimony produced by Browning. He was later convicted and hanged. In reviewing the record of the case, Chief Justice John Holt thoughtfully observed: "People should advise well before filing such actions." Good advice.

Obviously, not every defamation plaintiff ends up at the end of a rope. But people who sue for slander and libel do tend to discover, to their surprise and discomfort, that they have assumed the role of a defendant. A charge has been made against them, they have sued to prove the charge false, and the dynamics of the trial are reversed from the norm. The <u>plaintiff</u> can win only by proving that he or she is <u>not guilty</u> of the charges the <u>defendant</u> has made. That is an unpleasant public position to have to take, especially if one should happen to lose. Which is one reason many defamation actions are abandoned long prior to trial by plaintiffs with more mental acumen than the unfortunate Mr. Johnson.

28.

AN AMERICAN LAWYER DOES HIS JOB

"The plain English is, Gentlemen, they were a motley rabble of saucy boys, Negroes and Mulattoes, Irish teagues and outlandish jacktars."

John Adams, defending the British soldiers who killed American citizens in the Boston Massacre, 1770.

When we were in grade school, we learned about the Boston Massacre. We were told that on March 5, 1770, a squadron of British soldiers brutally gunned down five citizens of Boston. The Massacre was identified as the opening skirmish of the Revolutionary War. A Paul Revere engraving freezes the scene in the national memory: a British officer giving his troops the command to fire into a harmless crowd.

No one ever told us, however, what happened to the perpetrators of the dreadful killings. The interesting reality is that they were tried in a Boston court on charges of murder. The far more interesting reality is the identity of their chief defense counsel—none other than Founding Father John Adams. Adams accepted the case because no other experienced Boston lawyer would. He did so after much agonizing and floor-pacing, during which his political future must have passed before his eyes many times.

He did not provide a perfunctory defense for his alien clients. He introduced evidence that the crowd had taunted the soldiers unmercifully, calling them "lobsters" and "cowards", and had posed an imminent threat of physical violence. The scene described in his final argument bore no resemblance to the one depicted in the Paul Revere engraving:

> The soldiers were chained to the spot by the command of their officer. They were bound by their oath to obedience.... They were a peaceful assembly and the people attacking them were, by every principle of law, a mob.

To the horror of most courtroom observers, he proceeded to convert the American victims of the Massacre into the villains of the piece:

> We have been entertained with a variety of phrases, to avoid calling this sort of people a mob. Some call them shavers, some call them geniuses. The plain English is, Gentlemen, they were a motley rabble of saucy boys, negroes and mulattos, Irish teagues and outlandish jacktars. And why we should scruple to call such a set of people a mob, I cannot conceive, unless the name is too respectable for them. The sun is not about to stand still or go out, nor the rivers to dry up, because there was a mob in Boston on the 5th of March that attacked a party of soldiers.

He asked his fellow Americans to rise above partisanship, and to perform the duty of a juror, which is simply to judge a case on its facts:

> Facts are stubborn things, and whatever may be our wishes, our inclinations, our passions, they cannot alter the state of facts in evidence.

The result was somewhat amazing, considering the circumstances. Two soldiers were convicted of the reduced charge of manslaughter, and six were acquitted of any wrongdoing. Most of Boston was outraged that Adams had performed his job with such unpatriotic fervor. The word "traitor" was spoken more than once in discussions of his argument. Adams' explanation was as honorable as his performance had been. If the world is to support America's cause, he said, "it must know that America is a civilized place, where even its adversaries can find justice".

All in all, it was a splendid beginning for the American legal system.

29.

THE MOST FATEFUL OMISSION FROM THE DECLARATION OF INDEPENDENCE

> "[King George III] has waged a cruel war against human nature, by assaulting a distant people and captivating and carrying them into this hemisphere."
>
> Thomas Jefferson, 1776.

Jefferson was sincere when he castigated King George for supporting the slave trade in an early draft of the Declaration of Independence. Jefferson himself owned inherited slaves, but he believed that slavery was a national curse that would ultimately destroy America. He was careful not to cast any blame on American pro-slavery factions, but that bit of hypocrisy did him no good. The South Carolina delegates said they would not support the Declaration unless the reference to slavery was removed.

The forced deletion foretold the Nation's fate. A fatal crack existed in the American culture, and for the first of many times, it was papered over with a thin tissue of concession. As that crack widened in future years, Americans desperately tried to bridge it with a series of precarious compromises. There was the Missouri Compromise, the Kansas/Nebraska Act, the Compromise of 1850, the Wilmont Proviso, and the Crittendon Compromise, all seeking to balance pro and anti-slavery forces—until finally, the Nation was forced to confront itself in civil war.

Jefferson saw it all coming, and more. His solution to the inexorable dilemma of slavery would have avoided a civil war, but it is shocking to modern sensibilities. He proposed the forced ex-patriation of all negroes to a distant colony to avoid what he saw as an inevitable Holocaust, pitting blacks against whites. When he submitted the proposal to the Virginia General Assembly in 1782, his fellow colonists turned it down—not out of altruism, but because they wanted to keep their slaves.

Jefferson saw race-mixing as the only alternative to ex-patriation, and race-mixing as unthinkable. He believed that integration would produce terrible strife: "Deep-rooted prejudices entertained by the whites; ten thousand recollections, by the blacks, of the injuries they have sustained; new provocations; the real distinctions which nature has made; and many other circumstances, will divide us into parties, and produce convulsions, which will probably never end, but in the extermination of the one or the other race."

But he also opposed integration because of what he saw as the inherent inferiority of the Negro. He took it for granted that whites were naturally more beautiful. "Are not the fine mixtures of red and white, the expressions of every passion by greater or less suffusions of color in the one, preferable to that eternal monotony, which reigns in the countenances, that immovable veil of black which covers the emotions of the other race? ... The circumstance of superior beauty is thought worthy attention in the propagation of our horses, dogs, and other domestic animals; why not in that of man?"

There was more: "[Negroes] have less hair on the face and body. They secrete less by the kidneys and more by the glands of the skin, which gives them a very strong and disagreeable odor ... They are more ardent after their females; but love seems with them to be more an eager desire, than a tender delicate mixture of sentiment and sensation. Their emotions are transient. Those numberless affections, which render it doubtful whether Heaven has given life to us in mercy or in wrath are less felt, and sooner forgotten with them."

His repudiation of slavery in the Declaration draft was not a cry for human equality, but a complaint about a terrible burden he thought had been imposed upon America. The solution to the evils of King George's slave trade was not to confer "the blessings of liberty" on a less fortunate race, but to send an inferior race "back to where it came from".

It is said that morality is relative to time and place. Still, it is hard to reconcile Jefferson's expressed sentiments about negroes with his immortal proclamation that "all men are created equal". It must have meant something different to him (and many succeeding generations) than it means to us. What word in the great statement do you suppose we don't understand in the way he did, "equal"—or "men"?

30.

THE NEAREST MISS ON A MOMENTOUS HISTORICAL PREDICTION

> "The second of July, 1776 will be the most memorable … in the history of America. I am apt to believe that it will be celebrated by succeeding generations as the great anniversary festival."
>
> John Adams to his wife Abigail on July 3, 1776.

Adams was like a musician playing a grand overture, who triumphantly strikes the wrong key. His misprediction <u>was</u> extremely logical. On July 2nd, the United Colonies had committed the first official act of independence by adopting a resolution stating that they were "and of a right ought to be free and independent states." Adams had no way of knowing that this action would be obscured by the bold eloquence of the yet-to-be-adopted, full blown Declaration on July 4th. If July 2nd <u>had</u> prevailed as the Nation's birthday, one of the great stories of American history would have been ruined: Adams' and Jefferson's nearly simultaneous deaths on July 4th, exactly fifty years later.

31.

THE MOST OVERRATED STATEMENT IN SUPPORT OF FREEDOM OF THE PRESS

"[W]ere it left to me to decide whether we should have a government without newspapers, or newspapers without government, I should not hesitate a moment to prefer the latter."

Thomas Jefferson in a letter to Edward Carrington, 1787.

No other statement by a Founding Father has been quoted so often by free press advocates. Jefferson's startling epigram has fed the myth that he was a great friend of the press, who believed that it should not be held accountable by government. Actually, he despised the press of his time far more than he admired it, and believed that it should be soundly punished for its excesses. In other correspondence, Jefferson wrote: "Nothing can now be believed which is seen in a newspaper. Truth itself becomes suspicious by being placed into that polluted vehicle", and "the man who never looks into a newspaper is better informed than he who reads them; inasmuch as he who knows nothing is nearer the truth than he whose mind is filled with falsehoods and error."

While many of his contemporaries, including James Madison, advanced the bold new theory that American citizens should never be punished for what they wrote about their government, Jefferson believed in strong enforcement of criminal libel laws against newspapers and for the most part "contributed only tired cliches"[2] to the free press debate. It is ironic that his attitude toward the press has been historically defined by one of the few statements he made which implies a radical position.

---

2   Levy, Jefferson and Civil Liberties, 55 (1963).

32.

KING GEORGE "MAKES UP" WITH AMERICA

"I have done nothing in the late contest but what I thought myself indispensably bound to do by the duty which I owed my people... The separation having been made, and having become inevitable, I have always said, as I say now, that I would be the first to meet the friendship of the United States as an independent power."

George III to John Adams, circa 1796.

When President Lyndon Johnson felt America sliding into a major war in Vietnam in early 1964 he consulted his principal foreign affairs mentor, Senator Richard Russell of Georgia. "What must I do?" he implored. "Pull back, Mr. President" Russell advised. "Down my way, we believe it's a bad idea to mess with another man's land."

It was good advice which powerful countries that invade small, supposedly weak countries have tended to ignore, to their sorrow and humiliation: the French in Algeria and Vietnam, the United States in Vietnam, the Soviets in Afghanistan and, of course, The U.S. in Iraq. The invasion is always easier than the never-graceful exit from the "other man's land". George III came closest in the latter respect than the leaders of the aforementioned powers. But, then, he lived in civilized times.

33.

THE MOST ASTOUNDING COURTROOM MIS-IDENTIFICATION OF A CRIMINAL DEFENDANT

"I am as well convinced as I can possibly be of anything in the world, that the defendant, now here, is the person who married me as Thomas Hoage. I then thought him, and still think him, the handsomest man I ever saw; how often have I combed those dear locks!"

Testimony of Catherine Hoage, 1801.

The prosecution of "Thomas Hoage" in Rockland County, New York, in 1801 was one of the strangest trials in American history. The indictment charged that, having married Susan Faesch on March 8, 1789, and not having divorced her, the defendant had married a woman named Catherine Secor on December 25, 1800, and was guilty of bigamy. The man on trial asserted the startling defense that, whatever Hoage's marital conduct may have been, he himself was innocent of bigamy—because he was not Thomas Hoage!

The first dramatic high point of the trial was Catherine Hoage's vivid identification of the defendant as her husband, Thomas, quoted above. The second was the testimony of Moses Anderson, a rebuttal witness for the prosecution. He stated that he had worked for Hoage in December, 1800 and had spent every Sunday at his house. He then looked at the man in the dock with a quizzical stare, and said:

> If he is Thomas Hoage, he has a scar on his forehead, which he told me was occasioned by the kick of a horse. He also had a small mark on his neck. He also had a scar under his foot, between his heel and the ball of his foot, occasioned,

as he said, by treading on a drawing knife. The scar is easy to be seen.

The defendant whispered something to his lawyer, who requested a recess and conferred with the prosecutor. When the court came back into session, the defendant was called to the stand. "Take off your shoes and show your feet to the jury," his lawyer quietly requested. The defendant unlaced and removed his shoes, then his socks and displayed his feet to his twelve fellow citizens. They were as unmarked as a newborn infant's bottom.

The man on trial was not the faithless Thomas Hoage, but the entirely innocent Joseph Parker of New York City. Although he had no known biological relationship to Hoage, he was nearly identical to him in appearance—a veritable dobbleganger. Catherine Hoage's face to face identification of her "own husband" had seemed irrefutable, but it had been conclusively refuted in an instant.

The case is almost factually unique, but the point it illustrates is not. Eye witness identification is a great instrument of injustice—perhaps more so than coerced or false confessions. This is because juries incorrectly regard it as the most reliable form of evidence and give it more weight than it deserves. After all, what could be more convincing than an objective witness' confident statement that the defendant is "the man"?

Prosecutors know better. Most of them have seen soft out of court identifications become rock hard in court, because of the psychological conditioning a trial provides. This conditioning process is memorialized in a prosecutor's joke:

Q: Do you see the man who robbed the bank in the courtroom today?
A: Yes.
Q: Where is he seated?
A: He is the nervous looking character sitting next to the guy in the twelve hundred dollar suit.

34.

THE POWER OF PLAGIARISM

"It is emphatically the province and duty of the Judicial Department to say what the law is.... So if a law be in opposition to the Constitution; if both the law and the Constitution apply to a certain case, so the court must decide the case conformably to the law, disregarding the Constitution; or conformably to the Constitution, disregarding the law; the court must decide which of these conflicting rules governs the case. This is the very essence of the judicial duty.

If, then, the courts are to regard the Constitution, and the Constitution is superior to any Act of the Legislature, the Constitution, not such ordinary Act must control the case to which they both apply."

Justice John Marshall in *Marbury v. Madison,* (1803).

* * * *

"The interpretation of the laws is the proper province and duty of the courts. It must, therefore, belong to them to ascertain (the Constitution's) meaning as well as the meaning of any particular Act proceeding from the Legislative body. If there would happen to be an irreconcilable variance between the two, that which has the superior obligation and validity, ought, of course, to be preferred; in other words, the Constitution ought to be preferred to the statute."

Federalist Papers No. 78, (1778).

Justice Marshall's famous pronouncement in *Marbury v. Madison* is the most important that ever appeared in a Supreme Court opinion. It gave the Court the authority to declare legislative acts unconstitutional—thereby wiping them off the books. This power of "judicial review" has made the Court the ultimate force in shaping America's social and legal policy. The Court has used it to end racial segregation, to construct sturdy protections for freedom of press and speech, to give reality to the Bill of Rights protections for people charged with crimes and to create high standards of fairness and justice in many other aspects of our lives. Since the adoption of the Constitution in 1791 until the present date, nothing has occurred that has so fundamentally defined and changed the functioning of our government as *Marbury v. Madison*.

Constitutional lawyers are, therefore, shocked to learn that the heart of the Marshall opinion is an <u>unattributed</u> paraphrase of No. 78 of the Federalist Papers, written twenty-five years earlier by Alexander Hamilton. Contemporary Justices and judges always cite their sources, often to the point of tedium. If the Marshall opinion had been written in 2003 instead of 1803, Federalist No. 78 would have been cited as authority and probably quoted in a footnote.

That would have been more candid but far less effective. It would have made the Marshall opinion read like a well-researched law review article—a creature of borrowed reasoning. Judicial immortality is conferred on wise pronouncements, not on careful scholarship. Much of the power of the Marshall opinion lies in its very lack of citations. He told the world what his Court believed and knew, not what they had learned in the library; without citations his words appeared as the natural wisdom they were.

Of course every intellectual insight comes, in a sense, from a library. "Original" thoughts are the deposit of forgotten, studied wisdom. But what early American judges understood and their modern successors apparently don't, is that undocumented and minimally documented ideas have the power of originality that over-documented ones do not. Citing <u>some</u> precedent and staying consistent with their general philosophy has become an increasingly important part of the process as the law has matured and evolved, but the people still like to think that the concepts that guide their lives represent the convictions of the justices who state them, not the fruit of an avid clerk's diligent research labors.

Just as *Marbury* is considered the foremost Supreme Court opinion, Oliver Wendell Holmes' dissenting opinion in *Lochner v. U.S.* (1905), is considered the Court's greatest dissent. It is the Gettysburg Address of Supreme Court opinions: short, unadorned and powerful in its very simplicity. It is no coincidence that Holmes' six hundred word essay cited not a single precedent. Like Marshall's opinion one hundred years before, Holmes' masterpiece derived much of its power from its Natural Law effect. Like Marshall, Holmes appeared to have summoned up first principles, not borrowed ones, and made his great opinion a thing unto himself.

Commenting recently upon the *Lochner* dissent, Seventh Circuit Judge Richard Posner noted that it was far from a model of judicial craftsmanship. "It is not logically organized, it does not join issues sharply with the majority, it is not scrupulous in its treatment of the majority or of precedent, it is not thoroughly researched, does not exploit the factual record ... It is unlikely that any contemporary Supreme Court justice would produce such an unannotated personalized piece of judicial philosophy." But Posner concluded, although Holmes' dissent may not qualify as a "good judicial opinion ... it is merely the greatest judicial opinion of the last hundred years. To judge it by the [usual] standards is to miss the point. It is a rhetorical masterpiece."

In the rare moments when Supreme Court justices are at their very best they realize that they are not merely scholars or analysts. They are appointed to be Philosopher Kings. Especially when dealing with novel questions about our fundamental law they are expected to tell us what they, not others, think and know and believe. Why else would we put them on the Court?

35.

THE MOST GROSSLY OVERRATED LINE BY A FAMOUS LEGAL ORATOR

"It is, sir, as I have said, a small college. And yet there are those who love it."

Daniel Webster, arguing the Dartmouth College case before the United States Supreme Court, 1818.

This mawkish little bromide is perhaps the most famous public utterance of America's most famous appellate lawyer. Webster uttered it toward the close of a four-hour argument in *Dartmouth College v. Woodward*, in which the Supreme Court held that the New Hampshire Legislature had acted unconstitutionally in converting Dartmouth into a State university. According to Justice Story,[3] "Many [in the courtroom] were dissolved in tears; many betrayed the most agitated mental struggles; many were sinking under exhausting efforts to conceal their own emotions."

Obviously, Webster's words have survived because they were delivered in an electrifying manner; they certainly did not win immortality on their own. Their very mawkishness is the greatest possible compliment to the speaker. If it had been anyone but Webster, Justice Story might have found himself describing tears of laughter.

---

3   Story was describing Webster's entire peroration, not specifically the small college statement. Much of the rest of it was even worse by modern standards; e.g., Sir, I know not how others may feel, but, for myself, when I see my Alma Mater surrounded like Caesar in the Senate House, by those who are reiterating stab upon stab, I would not, for this right hand, have her turn to me, and say.... And thou too, my son!

36.

GREATNESS IN DISGUISE

"My Dear Judge—The bearer of this is a young man who thinks he can be a lawyer. Examine him, if you want to. I have done so, and am satisfied. He's a good deal smarter than he looks to be."

Letter presented by Abraham Lincoln in support of his application for admission to the Illinois bar, (circa 1838).

Lincoln was admitted to the bar without examination.

37.

A LAWYER SHRINKS INTO A JUDGE

"[U]ntil the time comes when we can point without a blush to the language held in the Declaration of Independence, every friend of humanity will seek to lighten the galling chain of slavery."

Lawyer Roger Taney, 1819.

"[The phrase] 'all men are created equal' ... would seem to embrace the whole human family.... But it is too clear for dispute that the enslaved African race was not intended to be included."

Chief Justice Roger Taney, 1857.

There is a sad irony about the life of Roger Taney. He was born to be a superior lawyer and he became one of the best in our Nation's history. If he had anticipated what would happen to him in his old age, however, he might never have entered the legal profession.

His greatest triumph as a trial lawyer occurred in 1819, when he defended Reverend Jacob Gruber in a Maryland criminal court. Gruber was charged with inciting slaves to riot. He had, in essence, told a crowd of blacks that they were entitled to be treated as human beings.

The safest course might have been to placate the jury, but Taney chose instead to speak from his heart and to appeal to the jurors' idealism by invoking the Declaration of Independence. "Mr. Gruber did quote the language of our great Act of National Independence," he said, "and insisted on the principles contained in that venerated instrument ... While slavery continues, it is a blot upon our national character, and every real lover of freedom confidently hopes that it will be effectively, though it must be gradually, wiped away. Until the time comes when we can point without a blush to the language held in the

Declaration every friend of humanity will seek to lighten the galling chain of slavery."

Gruber was acquitted, and it was a happy moment in history. Taney had given "every friend of humanity" reason to hope that the promise of the Declaration of Independence might someday apply to all Americans. Tragically—unbelievably—it was Taney himself who 38 years later brought death to that dream.

In March of 1857, Chief Justice Roger Taney sat in the center of the Supreme Court bench, reading the opinion in *Dred Scott v. Sandford*. It was a decision destined to tear the country apart, and to destroy Taney's reputation as a moral and brilliant jurist. Scott was a slave who had traveled to a free territory and claimed that he had thereby become an American citizen. The ruling of the Supreme Court—authored by the one time defender of Reverend Jacob Gruber—was, simply, that such a thing was impossible. Slaves were not constitutionally people, hence could not become citizens, hence could not even bring suit in a United States court as Scott had attempted to do.

The words chosen by Taney to justify the decision were the antithesis of those he had used in defending Gruber so long ago. "At the time the Declaration of Independence came into being," he said, "slaves had for more than a century been regarded as beings of an inferior order, and altogether unfit to associate with the white race, either in social or political relations; and so far inferior that they had no rights that the white man was bound to respect…." These inferior beings, Taney concluded, were not considered equal in 1776, and, therefore, could not be treated as equals in 1857.

When Roger Taney went to bed that night, he had rendered the worst decision in Supreme Court history. The *Dred Scott* case damaged the Court's prestige for decades and brought the Civil War closer to reality. In a famous phrase, Taney's opinion was called "a blunder—a blunder worse than a crime". The reasons for the decision have been elaborately debated. It was said, for example, that Taney had actually tried to save the Republic from civil war, by resolving judicially that which could not be resolved politically. In human terms, it hardly mattered. In 1864 at the age of 87, Roger Taney died "publicly unlamented" by a people whose idealism he had calculatedly betrayed.

38.

BY THE LIGHT OF THE NON-EXISTENT MOON

Lincoln: "How, then, did you see the shooting."
Sovine: "By moonlight."

Abraham Lincoln's alleged cross-examination of a prosecution witness in an 1858 murder trial.

Abraham Lincoln's devastation of the lying witness Sovine is the most famous cross-examination in American history. People who know nothing else about our legal heritage have heard the story of the almanac and the moon that didn't shine.

The story goes that Abraham Lincoln once represented a man named Grayson, who was charged with shooting a man named Lockwood near a camp meeting. Sovine testified for the prosecution that he had been with Lockwood on the night in question, and dramatically identified Grayson as the man who had shot him. On cross-examination, Lincoln got Sovine to say that he had been able to see the murderer because of the brightness of the moon, and then produced a blue-covered almanac and offered it into evidence. He read an entry from it which stated that the moon had not been visible on the night of the murder until 1:00 a.m.—three hours after the murder occurred.

Lincoln then moved for Sovine's arrest, saying that "nothing but a motive to clear himself could have induced him to swear away so falsely the life of one who never did him any harm". Sovine was arrested and later confessed to the murder.

Like most really good stories, this one is more or less false. Even the names are wrong. In real life, the man Lincoln defended was one William "Duff" Armstrong who was supposed to have been involved in a fatal drunken brawl at a campground with one James "Pres" Metzker. Eyewitnesses said that Armstrong struck Metzker a mortal blow on the head with a weapon called a slungshot. Armstrong's defense was that it had been a fair fist fight without weapons. The star prosecution witness was a house painter named James Allen, who testified that he had clearly seen Armstrong strike Metzker with a slungshot. On cross-examination, Allen told Lincoln that he had been standing about forty feet from the fighting men, and that there had been a full moon which had shown "almost as bright as day ... about where the sun would be at ten o'clock in the day".

Lincoln quietly placed an almanac in evidence without reading from it. In his final argument, he read a passage from the almanac stating that there had been only a quarter moon on the night of the murder, and that the moon had been low in the sky, about an hour from setting when the murder occurred. He did not argue that the paleness of the moonlight would have prevented Allen from seeing the murder, only that Allen's inaccurate description of the moon made the other details of his testimony suspect.

Armstrong was acquitted, but it is unlikely that the phase of the moon had much impact on the verdict. The defendant himself said that there had been no moon that night, but admitted that the fight had been clearly visible to the spectators because of the candlelight from the liquor bar. Allen was not arrested, or suspected of any part in the alleged murder.

There is, of course, nothing surprising in any of this. Events involving famous people are inevitably "improved upon" in the re-telling, because popular history demands it. Once a reputation is made, it tends to grow by sheer momentum—the world assigns great deeds to great men, with or without their cooperation.

39.

A MEMORABLE SUPREME COURT ARGUMENT NO ONE REMEMBERS

"I am not afraid that you will underrate the importance of this case. It concerns the rights of the whole people. Such questions have generally been settled by armies, but since the beginning of the world no battle has ever been lost or won upon which the liberties of a nation were so distinctly staked as they are on the result of this argument."

Jeremiah Black in *ex parte Miliken*, March, 1866.

Lambdin Miliken was a confederate sympathizer who lived in Huntington, Indiana during the Civil War. He helped form the Sons of Liberty whose purpose was to organize resistance to the Union military drafts and to act as spies for the confederate cause. On October 5, 1864, he and other leaders of the organization were arrested by the Northern Army and tried before a military commission on what amounted to charges of treason. Miliken's lawyers argued that the tribunal had no jurisdiction because Indiana was not within any war zone and was therefore not subject to the authority of the Army. He lost his argument and was sentenced to death.

Believing that the case was too important for it to decide, the U.S. Circuit Court for the District of Indiana certified it to the Supreme Court. Miliken and his fellow petitioners were represented by a veritable covey of brilliant advocates. The main argument was presented by Jeremiah Black who had been a justice of the Supreme Court of Pennsylvania, a U.S. Attorney General and a Secretary of State.

The case was argued from March 5 to March 13, 1866. Such rhetorical festivals were common in important 19th Century Supreme Court cases, and many of the lawyers of that more eloquent age were good enough at their craft to keep the justices from falling asleep as they argued on and on and on. Even so, Black's performance was remarkable, perhaps unique, for its combination of virtuosity and sheer length. He spoke without intermission or pause for eight straight hours, without consulting a single note. The comment of an anonymous observer provides a sense of the brilliance of his speech. Despite its immense, unbroken duration, the man reported, "he presented an array of law, fact and argument with such remarkable force and eloquence as startled and bewildered those who listened to him".

Whether it was Black's awesome effort or the logic of the case, he and his colleagues were successful. A divided court held that the petitioners should be granted writs of *habeas corpus* and set free. The decision is a landmark in the history of the Great Writ, and in the development of individual liberties in America.

If Mr. Black had argued the *Miliken* case in 1965 instead of 1865 he would have found himself in a different universe. Whatever wisdom, learning and emotion he wanted to convey on behalf of his client, and in support of the gigantic issue at stake, would probably have been packed into a handy thirty minutes, much of it filled with questions from the Bench. That is the full extent of the opportunity most lawyers are given today to communicate personally with the Court. With rare exceptions modern lawyers are cut off, even in mid sentence, when that precious scintilla of time expires.

And why not? After all, the large cluster of Supreme Court clerks have ample time to read and analyze the written briefs lawyers file. Human to human communication, intellectual give and take, spontaneous exploration of the meaning of the case, are considered to be a relative waste of the Court's energies.

Does this shrinkage in the human dimensions of Supreme Court advocacy affect the quality of the decisions? Very likely so. For the case-deciders the process is more like reading a script than attending a play—let alone participating in a debate. But consider the advantage—if short, fractured arguments distance the Justices from the subjects of their decisions, it also gives them time to write longer and more complicated ones which are worthy of the abstract modern process of establishing our most important policy and law.

40.

THE SUPREME COURT'S BLOODIEST SELF-INFLICTED WOUND

"It is difficult to conceive what Act would take private property without process of law if [the Legal Tender] Act would not."

Legal Tender Cases, 1870.

"It would be anomalous for us to hold an act of Congress [the Legal Tender Act] invalid merely because we think its provisions harsh and unjust."

Legal Tender Cases, 1871.

The prestige of the U.S. Supreme Court is tenuous. The justices are nine Wizards of Oz, whose authority depends upon maintaining the public's suspension of disbelief. There is nothing extraordinary about most of them, except their luck in being appointed to the High Tribunal. We know this when we think about it, but we seldom do so, because their position requires us to presume them at least tolerably wise. When that presumption becomes weak, the rule of law is put at risk.

The worst time for the Court's prestige was in the middle of the 19th Century. The turmoil that produced the Civil War was reflected in the workings of the Court. In 1869, the Court was still recovering from the effects of the *Dred Scott* decision, which had attempted to solve the dilemma of slavery by a disreputable judicial decree. In order to prevent President Andrew Johnson, a southern sympathizer, from packing the Court to thwart reconstruction, Congress reduced the number of authorized justices from nine to seven. When Union General Ulysses S. Grant was elected president in 1869, the number was nimbly restored to nine.

Meanwhile, a vital group of cases had come before the Court. At issue was the validity of the Legal Tender Act of 1862, which authorized the federal government to issue paper money. In 1870, the seven justices then sitting decided by a vote of four to three that the Act was unconstitutional. The decision had a certain logic. The Constitution had given Congress the power only to "coin" money, saying nothing about printing paper money. Moreover, nothing about the constitutional convention of 1787 was clearer than the Framers' determination to prevent the issuance of paper money, and all the woes such currency had historically produced.

On the other hand, the decision was a disaster for the American economy. Practically every other enlightened country in the world possessed the authority to issue paper currency, and it was hard to conceive of an 1870 economy operating solely on metal coins. The Court was dead right in terms of the Framers' historical intent, and dead wrong in terms of the Nation's current welfare.

By an unfortunate stroke of fate, President Grant nominated Joseph Bradley and William Strong to fill the newly created vacancies on the Court on the very day the Legal Tender decision was announced. The Court then made the horrendous error of ordering <u>immediate</u> re-argument of the case. Within the year, the two new justices had joined the three former dissenters to reverse the prior decision, and restore life to the Act's still warm corpse.

All of these maneuverings had a predictable effect on the public. The decision itself was popular, but the deck-shuffling by which it had been reached was abhorred. President Grant's motives may have been—as he earnestly insisted— as pure as the straight whiskey he drank, but the public didn't believe it for a moment. A typical newspaper account predicted that the fiasco would "greatly aggravate the growing contempt for what has long been the most respected … department of our government, its Judiciary". This turned out to be the journalistic understatement of the decade.

In the rear-view mirror of history, the far away past looks more placid than it was. When we think of crises experienced by the Supreme Court, we think of F.D.R.'s court packing plan in the 1930's, or the hatred generated by the 1950's desegregation cases. Gone is the memory of 1871, when the Court made a good decision, but made it with very bad timing, and suffered a grievous self-inflicted wound. It took the Court another decade and a half to recover its prestige—so fragile is the fabric of our rule of law.

41.

A VERY SMALL VERDICT IN A VERY LARGE CASE

"We, the jury, find for the plaintiff, and assess his damages at one farthing."

Whistler v. Ruskin, 1878.

In the 19th Century trials were a form of popular entertainment. The public jammed courtrooms in particularly interesting cases, listening for grisly details, elevated oratory and witty repartee. Libel trials were particular crowd favorites, and the ones involving famous people were smash hits. The lawyers and witnesses were expected to perform with one eye on a favorable verdict and the other on the entertainment of the audience, and they usually obliged.

The most famous of the libel trials were Oscar Wilde's prosecution of the Marquis of Queensbury in 1890 and James Whistler's suit against John Ruskin in 1878. They both featured clever, colorful testimony by a gifted artist. There was one stark difference between them, however: Wilde's case ended in tragedy, Whistler's ended in farce.

The basis of the Whistler suit was a criticism Ruskin had published about one of his paintings, which read:

> Sir Coutts Lindsay [who had exhibited the Whistler painting] ought not to have admitted works into the gallery in which the ill educated conceit of the artist so nearly approached the aspect of willful imposture. I have seen, and heard, much of cockney impudence before now; but never expected to hear a coxcomb ask two hundred guineas for flinging a pot of paint in the public's face.

As a witness, Whistler performed with the wit and charm that were expected of him. When Ruskin's lawyer asked him on cross-examination how long it had taken him to paint "Nocturne in Black and Gold", the picture Ruskin had criticized, Whistler replied:

A. To knock off that nocturne; as well as I remember, about a day.
Q. Only a day?
A. I may have put a few more touches to it the next day, if the painting were not dry.
Q. Oh, two days! The labor of two days, then, is that for which you ask two hundred guineas!
A. No; I ask it for the knowledge of a lifetime. (Applause).

* * * *

Q. (Referring to the painting.) The prevailing color is blue?
A. Perhaps.
Q. Are those figures on the top of the bridge intended for people?
A. They are just what you like.
Q. Is that a barge beneath?
A. Yes. I am very encouraged at your perceiving that.

* * * *

Q. Then you mean, Mr. Whistler, that the initiated on technical matters might have no difficulty in understanding your work. But do you think now that you could make me see the beauty of that picture?
Court record: The witness paused, and, examining attentively [the lawyer's] face and looking at the picture alternatively, said, after apparently giving the subject much thought, while the court waited in silence for his answer:
A. No! Do you know I fear it would be as hopeless as for a musician to pour his notes into the ear of a deaf man.

The farcical ending came with the jury's verdict. Whistler had sued for a thousand pounds, a very substantial sum in those days. The jury returned a verdict for the plaintiff, but set damages at one farthing—the smallest unit of the English currency system. Whistler's supporters said that the verdict reflected how little his reputation had been damaged. His detractors said that it reflected how little his reputation was worth.

42.

LETTING DEFENDANTS OFF ON SPELLING AND GRAMMAR

"The verdict is in a form unknown to the law, and has no force and effect. The conviction is reversed and the indictment is dismissed."

Texas Court of Appeals, setting aside a conviction because the jury had returned a verdict of "guily" instead of "guilty", 1886.

There is a widespread belief that freeing criminals on the basis of legal technicalities is a modern phenomenon. Nothing could be further from the truth. At the art of capricious leniency, we of the Twentieth Century are novices and our ancestors were the masters.

This was especially true of Nineteenth Century Texas justice. The flagrant example quoted above was merely the worst of a very bad lot. Its total idiocy is underlined by a later decision by the same court <u>affirming</u> a verdict of "guity". In 1887, a law journal complained that the Texas Court of Appeals "seems to have been organized to overrule and reverse". The article pointed out that the Court had, during its thirteen year existence, reversed 1604 criminal cases, while affirming only 882. Like the above example, many of the reversals were based on misspellings and misphrasings of indictments and verdicts, which had nothing to do with procedural fairness, or guilt and innocence.

This obsession with precision in the phrasing of criminal charges was not confined to Texas. With only slight exaggeration, Abraham Lincoln told of an Illinois judge who would sentence a man to death for blowing his nose in public, but would quash the indictment if it failed to state which hand he had done it with. A 19th Century North Carolina opinion dismissed a murder indictment because it did not describe the length of the fatal wounds.

These practices were imported from England. For centuries, the one clear right an English defendant had was that the charges against him be grammatically pure. English courts subjected indictments to incredible standards of precision. An indictment that referred to "a boot" was no good if it meant "a shoe"; a reference to "sheep" was assumed to mean living sheep and could not be applied to dead ones; if the indictment charged that the defendant had stolen animals, it must state that he "drove or led them away" rather than using equivalent language. It was imperative that the indictment conclude with the statement that the defendant's crime was committed "against the peace and dignity of the King" (or "of our Lady the Queen"), and the omission of that magic phrase was fatal.

Whatever complaints may be made about the technicalities of modern criminal justice, they at least attempt to relate decisions to some practical reality. That cannot be said of the decisions of yesteryear which permitted grammar to control justice. If the critics of modern judicial "liberalism" had to put up with the loopholes spun by the old courts of Texas and England, they might well burn a few courthouses down.

43.

A MOST LETHAL CROSS-EXAMINATION

Russell: "Still locked up, hermetically sealed in your own bosom?"

Pigott: "No, because it has gone away out of my bosom, whatever it was."

Sir Charles Russell, 1887.

One of the most brutally effective cross-examinations in English history was Sir Charles Russell's destruction of a witness named Pigott in the "Parnell Papers" treason hearing in 1887. Pigott was the main witness against Charles Parnell, a member of Parliament who was accused in published letters of plotting the overthrow of English rule in Ireland. Pigott claimed that the accusations were true. As Parnell's counsel, Russell had been handed a gift from the gods—a letter Pigott had written to a Catholic archbishop before the accusatory letters became public. The letter warned that certain "proceedings" were under way to destroy Parnell's influence in Parliament. Pigott wrote that he would "defeat" those "proceedings" if the Archbishop wished him to do so.

Russell did not just confront the witness with the letter and insist that it undermined his testimony that the accusations against Parnell were true. He figuratively fed the letter to Pigott, paragraph by paragraph, until Pigott figuratively choked on it. The climax of the devastating examination was as follows:

Russell: (Handing Pigott the letter) Is that your letter? Do not bother to read it; tell me if it is your letter ... do not trouble to read it.
Pigott: Yes, I think it is.
Russell: Have you any doubt of it?
Pigott: No.
Russell: (Reading) My Lord: ... I wish to say that I have been made aware of the details of certain proceedings that are in preparation

	with the object of destroying the influence of the Parnellite Party in Parliament. (To Pigott) What were the certain proceedings that were in preparation?
Pigott:	(I do not recollect.
Russell:	(Turn to My Lords and repeat the answer.
Pigott:	(I do not recollect …
Russell:	(Did it refer to the incriminatory letters among other things?
Pigott:	(Oh, at that date … no.
Russell:	(Now you go on (reading) "I cannot enter more fully into details than to state that the proceedings referred to consist in <u>the publication of certain statements</u> purporting to prove the complicity of Mr. Parnell himself, and some of his supporters, with murders and outrages in Ireland …
	((I ask whether you did not intend to refer—not solely, I suggest, but among other things—to the letters, as being the matter which would prove complicity or purport to prove complicity.
Pigott:	((Reversing his prior testimony) Yes, I may have had that in mind …
Russell:	(You believe these letters to be genuine?
Pigott:	(I do.
Russell:	(And did at the time?
Pigott:	(Yes.
Russell:	((Reading) "And I will assure Your Grace that I am also able to point out how these designs may be successfully combated and finally defeated." Now, if these documents were genuine documents, and you believed them to be such, how were you able to assure His Grace that you were able to point out how the design might be successfully combated and finally defeated …
Pigott:	(I cannot conceive really.

The witness was trapped in a terrible testimonial dilemma. He could not continue to state—as he reluctantly had—that his letter referred to the Parnell letters without admitting that the charges contained in them were false, since he had told the archbishop he could "defeat them". How could he honorably "defeat" the charges if they were true? Having trapped his prey, Russell proceeded to skin, cook and devour it:

Russell:	(Oh, try. You must really try.
Pigott:	(I cannot.
Russell:	(Try.
Pigott:	(I cannot.
Russell:	(Try....
Pigott:	(I must have had something else in mind which I cannot at present recollect—I must have had other charges.
Russell:	(What charges?
Pigott:	(I do not know. That is what I cannot tell you.
Russell:	(If it appears to you clearly that you had not the letters in mind, what had you in your mind?
Pigott:	(t must have been something far more serious.
Russell:	(What was it?
Pigott:	(I cannot tell you. I have no idea.
Russell:	(It must have been something far more serious than the letters?
Pigott:	(Far more serious.
Russell:	(Can you give My Lords any clue of the most indirect kind as to what it was?
Pigott:	(I cannot.
Russell:	(Or from whom you heard it?
Pigott:	(No.
Russell:	(Or when you heard it?
Pigott:	(Or when I heard it.
Russell:	(Or where you heard it?
Pigott:	(Or where I heard it.
Russell:	(Have you ever mentioned this fearful matter—whatever it is—to anyone?

Pigott:	(No.
Russell:	(Still locked up, hermetically sealed in your own bosom?
Pigott:	(No, because it is gone away out of my bosom, whatever it was.

Parnell was exonerated. Pigott fled to Europe, and sent back a letter confessing his perjury. When the police came to his Madrid hotel room to arrest him, he retired to the bedroom and blew his brains out with a pistol.

Now, <u>that's</u> a cross-examination.

44.

A TRAGIC CASE OF TESTIMONIAL SUICIDE

Wilde: "He was a particularly plain boy. He was unfortunately very ugly. I pitied him for it."

Oscar Wilde, testifying in a prosecution for libel against the Marquis of Queensbury, 1890.

Oscar Wilde performed brilliantly as a witness in the libel prosecution he brought against the Marquis of Queensbury in 1890 for publicly accusing him of being a "sodomite". As the greatest wit of his time, he was uniquely qualified for the verbal combat of a trial. His gift for repartee, which had demolished many a social adversary, was readily adaptable to the courtroom. If his cross-examination had been a baseball game, he would have won by a score of, perhaps, 30 to 1.

Unfortunately for Wilde, a cross-examination is more like a boxing match than a baseball game. It is important to do well in the early rounds, but what really matters is how you finish. A single stunning blow can cancel hours of fancy verbal footwork and well aimed verbal punches. So it was with Wilde.

Believing that the jury would find Wilde's beliefs morally offensive, Queensbury's lawyer Edward Carson questioned him about a series of sayings he had published in a Saturday Review article. It soon became clear that Carson was badly overmatched:

> Carson (reading): "Religions die when they are proved to be true." Is that true?
>
> Wilde: Yes; I hold that. It is a suggestion toward a philosophy of the absorption of religion by science, but it is too big a question to go into now.
>
> Carson: Do you think that is a safe axiom to put forward for the philosophy of the young?
>
> Wilde: Most stimulating.

Carson: "If one tells the truth one is sure, sooner or later, to be found out?"

Wilde: That is a pleasing paradox, but I do not set a very high store on it as an axiom.

Carson: Is that good for the young?

Wilde: Anything is good for the young that stimulates thought, in whatever age.

Carson: Whether moral or immoral?

Wilde: There is no such thing as morality or immorality of thought. There is immoral emotion.

Carson: "A truth ceases to be true when more than one person believes in it."

Wilde: Perfectly. That would be my metaphysical definition of truth, something so personal that the same truth could never be appreciated by two minds.

* * * *

Carson then proceeded to question Wilde about a letter he had written to Lord Alfred Douglas, Queensbury's son and Wilde's supposed paramour:

Carson: Suppose a man who was not an artist had written this letter, would you say it was a proper letter?

Wilde: A man who was not an artist could not have written that letter.

Carson: Can I suggest, for the sake of your reputation, that there is nothing very wonderful in this: "Red rose-leaf lips of yours?"

Wilde: A great deal depends on the way it is read.

Carson: "Your slim gilt soul walks between passion and poetry." Is that a beautiful phrase?

Wilde: Not as you read it, Mr. Carson. You read it very badly.

* * * *

Carson then turned to Wilde's social life:

> Carson [referring to an all male party Wilde had attended]: Did you drink champagne yourself?
>
> Wilde: Yes; iced champagne is a favorite drink of mine ... Strongly against my doctor's orders.
>
> Carson: Never mind your doctor's order, Sir.
>
> Wilde: I never do.

Having failed to win a single battle, Carson suddenly won the war. He had been questioning Wilde about a young servant boy Wilde had known at Oxford, and Wilde had been turning his insinuations aside with his usual deftness. Abruptly, Carson asked: "Did you ever kiss him?" Wilde thoughtlessly responded with a deadly implied admission: "He was a particularly plain boy. He was unfortunately very ugly. I pitied him for it." The courtroom turned to ice. After so much brilliance, Wilde had revealed himself in three short sentences. The arrogance that had made him so good on cross-examination had suddenly made him look very, very bad to the Victorian jury.

45.

AN UNANSWERABLE FINAL ARGUMENT

"Can this Court sentence the prisoner to half of his natural life? Will it sentence him to half a minute or half the days of Methuselah?"

William Frederick Howe, 1893.

William Frederick Howe (1829–1902), and his partner Abraham Henry Hummel (1850–1926) were masters of the art of "getting defendants off on technicalities". The firm of Howe and Hummel had a monopoly on the criminal business of New York City in the latter 19th Century that was never equaled, before or since. Their permanent clients included Mother Mandlebaum, New York's preeminent fence and the army of thieves who supplied her; General Abe Greenthald Sheeney who headed a nationwide syndicate of pickpockets; Charles McLaughlin who headed a gang of forgerers; and the Whyos, an organization of thugs and killers that was perhaps the toughest of all the Nineteenth Century gangs.

Howe and Hummel prospered by sheer cunning. While their contemporaries at the bar relied upon evidence and eloquence to defend their clients, they searched for loopholes. Although they were looked down on as shysters, their mode of practice required real talent, not unlike that of a good park bench chess player. The loopholes they found in criminal statutes were real, and often impossible to refute, even though unintended by the legislature and absurd in their effects. Howe's defense of a man named Reilly on a charge of attempted arson was probably the most absurdly logical argument he ever made. Despite his best back alley efforts, his client had been convicted of attempted arson and faced a stiff jail sentence. Howe had a formidable last card to play. After listening to the prosecutor's plea for long-term confinement, Howe rose and gravely approached the bench. "The sentence for <u>attempted</u> arson", he reminded the judge, "is <u>half</u> the maximum imposed by law for the actual commission of the crime of arson". The judge nodded curtly. "The penalty for arson is <u>life</u> imprisonment," Howe went on. "If the court were to determine a sentence for Reilly, he would have to determine half a life." He had caught the judge's attention. "Scripture tells us that we know not the day nor the hour of our departure" he continued. "Can this court sentence the prisoner to half of his natural life? Will it sentence him to half a minute, or half the days of Methuselah?" Having no answer to these unanswerable questions, the court amazingly set Mr. Reilly free. (Surely there was a more practical solution to this theoretical quandary— perhaps some sort of an actuarial yardstick—but none seems to have occurred to the judge or prosecutor.)

Howe's discovery of the metaphysical impossibility of applying New York's sentencing law to attempted arson was brilliant, but it did not represent the apex of his career. That came a few years later when he and his partner discovered a technical error in New York's jailing procedures, which they used to empty the prison on Blackwell's Island of two hundred and forty of the three hundred and sixty prisoners being housed there.

Viewed from the distance of a hundred years, the machinations of Howe and Hummel have an amusing quality, like the antics of the lawyers in a Dickens novel. But they raise a serious issue that has always plagued the legal system, and plagues it still today: How can general laws enacted on behalf of decency avoid manipulation on behalf of the corrupt? Of course, the answer is they can't. Fairness requires generality, and generality inevitably creates specific loopholes, metaphysical and otherwise, for those with the skill to find them.

46.

THE MOST TELLING COMMENT ON JUDICIAL TENURE BY A SUPREME COURT JUSTICE

"A dirtier day's work I never did in my life."

Supreme Court Justice Steven Field, 1896.

Field was a towering figure on the United States Supreme Court for more than 34 years. Early in his tenure, the Court was faced with an internal crisis. Justice Robert Grier had suffered a stroke which deprived him of much of his mental capacity, but he continued to serve. Field and some of his colleagues went to Grier and convinced him to resign, averting a possible constitutional crisis.

Years later Field—now 83 and failing in mental capacity—posed a similar dilemma for the Court and Country. In an ironic reprise of history, Justice John Marshal Harlen approached him and suggested that he resign. When Field reacted angrily, Harlen reminded him that he himself had once asked Justice Grier to step down. "Yes," Field bitterly replied, "and a dirtier day's work I never did in my life."

The anecdote is funny, but it illustrates a serious paradox of our legal system: we want our judges to be free to exercise their power without concern for selfish advantage or disadvantage; we confer this freedom by giving them lifetime tenure; and that tenure gives them the ability to act with unrestrained selfishness if they chose to do so. This can be dangerous, because power begets a taste for power. The young Field saw Grier's continued tenure on the bench as a problem; the old Field saw his own continued tenure as a prerogative. He had come to view his public service as a personal right.

Such attitudes produce willful decisions, as well as long tenures. Judging becomes equated with personal viewpoint, and justice dies. The tenure system that frees judges to follow principle, licenses them to ignore it. Like Justice Harlen, we see the problem clearly—but we don't know how to cure it.

47.

THE MOST COLORFUL REPUDIATION OF A SUPREME COURT JUSTICE BY THE PRESIDENT WHO APPOINTED HIM

"I could carve out of a banana a judge with more backbone than that."

President Theodore Roosevelt denouncing Justice Oliver Wendell Holmes, 1904.

Arguably, the most important action taken by Theodore Roosevelt as president was the appointment of Oliver Wendell Holmes to the U.S. Supreme Court. Holmes was the most influential American judge of the Twentieth Century. He had the mind of a philosopher and the pen of a poet, and his opinions had a force and lucidity that we never see anymore. He set the course for much of American constitutional law, investing it with a skeptical humanism that has served us well.

How did T.R. feel about his great judge? Not to put too fine a point on it, he was disgusted by him. It is possible that Henry II felt better about his appointment of Archbishop Thomas Becket than Roosevelt did about Holmes.

It was fated from the beginning that Roosevelt would not be able to comprehend or tolerate Holmes on the Court. T.R. was too thorough a politician. The purpose of government was to exercise power, he thought, and the purpose of power was to further interests you believed in—or for other reasons favored. Holmes lived in a cooler, more elevated climate. He saw the same contending factions Roosevelt saw, but his purpose was to define the boundaries of their battles, not to enter the battles himself.

In making the unflattering comparison between Holmes's spine and a banana, T.R. had specific reference to Holmes' dissenting opinion in *Northern*

Securities Company v. United States, but the remark was a more or less accurate summary of Roosevelt's general attitude toward the Yankee from Olympus. In *Northern Securities*, Holmes expressed the belief that the "moneyed interests" T.R. so avidly opposed should have the same freedom to merge with one another that the working people Roosevelt so avidly supported had to picket. What was philosophical consistency to Holmes was political betrayal to Roosevelt.

As devastating as the "banana spine" comment seems, it was not original. Roosevelt had previously referred to President William McKinley, his predecessor in office, as "having no more backbone than a chocolate eclair". T.R.'s talent for imagery was limited, but he made the most of what he had.

48.

THE LOUDEST BACKFIRE OF A COURTROOM ARGUMENT

"No man who ever knew the meaning of the word 'freedom' ever attached the word 'legal' to it."

Clarence Darrow, 1920.

In 1920, Clarence Darrow appeared in an Illinois courtroom defending a number of Communists accused of violating the Illinois Espionage Act. The prosecutors made the mistake of trying to commit the jurors to the empty principle of "legal freedom"—meaning whatever freedom was permitted by the Espionage Act itself. They learned a devastating lesson about the art of counter-punching. His juices flowing, Darrow responded by addressing the jury thusly:

> What is "legal freedom".... No man who ever knew the meaning of the word "freedom" ever attached to it the word "legal". Freedom is freedom, and nothing is done by a government that is not legal; and men in the past who had their tongues pulled out, who were pierced with red-hot irons, who were boiled in oil, who were tied to stakes, who were bent on the rack and tortured until they died, who had every limb torn from them, who had their nails pulled out and splinters run into their flesh, all were enjoying "legal freedom" while they were tortured and killed. That is what you will enjoy if, in this Country of ours, the evil forces back of this prosecution can have their way and provide their kind of freedom.

Whew!
Second prize in this category goes to Daniel Webster, the best American trial lawyer of the 19th Century—as Darrow was of the 20th. Captain Joseph White of Salem, Massachusetts, had been murdered as he lay asleep on a May night in 1830. White was an extremely wealthy citizen of Salem, Massachusetts, and

the motive for his murder had to do with inheritance. The Commonwealth charged that Frank and Joseph Knapp had paid one Richard Crownshield a thousand dollars to commit the murder. Joseph had agreed to testify against his brother, but he threatened the collapse of the case at the last minute by refusing to appear as a witness. The Commonwealth had the next best thing to testimony, however; it had the magic of special prosecutor Daniel Webster.

In their final arguments, the defense lawyers made the natural mistake of emphasizing their client's innocence. This gave Webster an undoubtedly pre-planned retaliatory opportunity, similar to the "legal freedom" opportunity Darrow exploited in the espionage case. He began by agreeing with the defense that the jury's duty was to protect "the innocent". "But who are the innocent, whom the law should protect?" he asked. (Oh, ohh!)

> Gentlemen, Joseph White was <u>innocent</u>. They are <u>innocent</u> who, having lived in fear of God through the day, wish to sleep in His peace through the night, in their own bed. The law has established that those who live quietly may sleep quietly; that they who do no harm may feel no harm. The gentlemen can think of none that are <u>innocent</u>, except the prisoner at the bar, not yet convicted. Is a proven conspirator to murder <u>innocent</u>? Are the Crownshields and the Knapps <u>innocent</u>? What is <u>innocence</u>? How deep stained with blood—how reckless in crime—how deep in depravity may it be, and yet remain <u>innocent</u>?

When facing counter-punchers such as these it might be wiser for their opponents to simply waive argument. Arguing only seems to inspire the punchers.

49.

A CELEBRATED TESTIMONIAL DISTORTION

"My opinion is that [the bullet] is consistent with being fired from [Sacco's] pistol."

Captain Proctor, testifying in the Sacco and Vanzetti trial, July, 1921.

This crucial testimony in America's most infamous murder trial was a wicked piece of deception. The trial judge believed that Proctor had identified Sacco's pistol as the murder weapon, and so instructed the jury. The judge and jury had been intentionally misled. An affidavit later signed by Proctor revealed that "is consistent with being fired" did not mean "was fired". The affidavit stated: "Had I been asked the direct question whether I had any affirmative evidence whatever that this so-called mortal bullet had passed through this particular Sacco's pistol, I should have answered then, as I do now without hesitation, in the negative."

The prosecutor and Proctor had, of course, carefully contrived the testimony in advance, knowing that it would probably be misunderstood. Despite the outraged protestations of distinguished lawyers across the land, the Massachusetts judicial system would not grant the defendants a new trial and sent two probably innocent men to their deaths.[4] The most distressing characteristic of Proctor's testimony is not its deceptiveness or even its cruelty, but its utter lack of uniqueness. Unfortunately, it is distinguished from a thousand similar courtroom deceptions only by its notoriety.

---

4   There were serious defects in the trial other than Proctor's testimony.

50.

THE WORST ADVICE ABOUT A SUPREME COURT APPOINTMENT

"There is a United States District Judge of proper age, Learned Hand. He is an able judge and a hard worker. I appointed him on Wickersham's recommendation and he turned out to be a wild Roosevelt man and progressive.... If promoted to our Bench, he would most certainly herd with Brandeis and be a dissenter. I think it would be risking too much to appoint him."

Letter from Chief Justice William Howard Taft to President Warren Harding (circa 1922).

Nothing Taft ever wrote, including a mass of undistinguished judicial opinions, inflicted as much damage upon the American legal system as this petty political message. His pique was understandable—the subject of his remarks had supported Roosevelt against him in the 1912 presidential election—but, politics aside, Learned Hand would have brought greatness to the United States Supreme Court. Many believe that he was, simply, the best American judge of this century.

"[Hand is] universally acknowledged as the greatest living judge in the English-speaking world," wrote Federal District Judge Charles Wyzanski. "No oracular gifts are required for prophecy that when the history of American law in the first half of this century comes to be written, four judges will tower above the rest—Holmes, Brandeis, Cardozo, and Learned Hand," wrote Federal Circuit Judge Henry Friendly. "No other judge has contributed so much of enduring value to his civilization," wrote Federal Circuit Judge Jerome Frank. "Unquestionably first among American judges," wrote the *Harvard Law Review* in 1947. "The Great Judge" was the title of an article about Hand in *Life* magazine on November 4, 1946.

Taft's ignorant letter was a melancholy case of a dwarf tripping a giant, to the lasting detriment of American Justice.

51.

AN ANTI-CLIMACTIC ENDING TO A CELEBRATED CASE

"We see nothing to be gained by prolonging the life of this bizarre case. On the contrary, we think the peace and dignity of the state, which all criminal prosecutions are brought to redress, will be better conserved by the entry of a *nolle prosequi* (dismissal). Such a course is suggested to the Attorney General."

Tennessee Supreme Court in *State v. Scopes*, (1926).

The Scopes "monkey" trial in Dayton, Tennessee was perhaps the most famous American courtroom battle of the 20th Century. The defendant John Scopes was an idealistic young teacher who taught biology in the local high school. He defied a state statute which outlawed the teaching of evolution, and was indicted and prosecuted. He was defended by the titan lawyer Clarence Darrow who was opposed by the titan lawyer William Jennings Bryan. The climax of the trial was Darrow's cross-examination of Bryan, in which he destroyed his great adversary and perhaps hastened his post-trial death.

All of this is well-known. Surprisingly, what is not generally known is the final outcome of the case. Was Scopes acquitted or convicted? Was the state's "monkey" law upheld on appeal or declared invalid? Was Scopes' conviction, if any, affirmed or reversed?

The answers are disappointing, which is probably why they are not widely known. Scopes was convicted—undramatically—after Darrow, having made the speeches he had come to make, conceded his guilt, reserving the right to appeal the statute's constitutionally. The statute was upheld by the Tennessee Supreme Court, but the Court reversed Scopes' conviction on the ground that the judge, not the jury, had imposed the one hundred dollar fine. The reversal was absurd, since one hundred dollars was the smallest fine the jury could have imposed, and the judge's imposition of it could not have been harmful to the defendant.

Most absurdly of all, the Court effectively discouraged the Attorney General from further pursuing the case, treating it as merely a "bizarre" nuisance. This ensured that one of the most important trials in American history would have no official result. So far as the law was concerned, the case had never existed.

No one was punished or vindicated by the judicial system. The punishments and vindications were all performed by the press, and by the public's understanding of the great event through the press. The Great Monkey Trial demolished Tennessee's anti-evolution statute, and stopped the Creationist Movement cold, not because the case accomplished those results, but because the public perceived that it had done so.

What the people remembered about the case was not Scope's guilty plea or the Supreme Court's learned decision validating the law. They remembered Darrow's devastation of Bryan's literal biblical beliefs, as derisively reported by the press, led by the acerbic H.L. Mencken.

As has frequently been true of 20th Century American justice, what happened in court mattered less than what happened in the minds of the people. Almost no one knows that the much ridiculed *Scopes* case actually upheld the Monkey law.

52.

AN INELEGANT EXPLANATION OF A DECISION BY AN ELOQUENT JUSTICE

"Three generations of imbeciles are enough."

Justice Oliver Wendell Holmes, in *Buck v. Bell*, 1927.

With memorable terseness, the Yankee from Olympus authorized the forced sterilization of a woman of exceptionally low intelligence. Holmes' striking phrase stuck in the memories of admirers and foes alike. The writing style that made him famous here did him in. An offensive decision, which might have been forgotten, was assured immortality by the succinctly crude manner in which he announced it. A sloppy writer would have fared much better in history.

53.

A POETIC DESCRIPTION OF THE MODERN TREND OF JUDICIAL DECISION-MAKING

"Where is the wisdom that we have lost in knowledge;
Where is the knowledge that we have lost in information?"

T.S. Eliott, 1930's.

Eliott was describing life in general, but he might have been describing the American judicial system. Our system began with the stable clarity of wisdom, and has advanced to the flexible incoherence of informational overload.

Our first and greatest Chief Justice, John Marshall, dealt in unfootnoted wisdom. In one of his most famous statements, he told lawyers "We must never forget that it is a Constitution we are expounding, intended to last for the ages". He meant that constitutional interpretation should rest on broad self-evident propositions that meet the test of time. Marshall's conclusions were not, of course, as self-evident as the power of his language made them seem, but the appearance was the substance.

Our greatest 20th Century Justice, Oliver Wendell Holmes, fought the battle of wisdom versus knowledge. The main constitutional conflict of his time was over the power of government to regulate business. Most of the justices Holmes served with thought that government regulation of business was severely limited by the Due Process Clause, because they equated "due process" with a free market. The "survival of the fittest" philosophy, popular with economists of the time, was, in their view, constitutionally mandated. Holmes insisted that the Constitution did not incorporate any particular economic theory, and that constitutional judging should be guided by the wisdom of judicial restraint. Within very broad limits, he said, the courts must permit the public and private sectors to deal with one another unfettered by court-dictated economic doctrine. In the activist constitutional period which began in the mid-1950's, knowledge was often predominate in Supreme Court decision-making. The great foundation case was *Brown v. Board of Education*, in which school desegregation was declared illegal. Although color-blind treatment of citizens was a policy of moral wisdom, the Court found it necessary to support its decision with empirical knowledge. The most famous part of the *Brown* decision is footnote 13, which presented the findings of sociologist Gunner Myrdal regarding the psychological effects of segregation upon minorities. The footnote gave the *Brown* decision an academic cast that provided its critics with something to attack besides the basic moral issue. The Court might have done better to stick with moral wisdom—but then, again, maybe not.

In recent years, the Court—along with the rest of the Country—has joyously joined the information age. The results have often been confusion breeding confusion.

In 1972, the Supreme Court rendered the longest decision in its history, deciding, by a five to four vote, to outlaw state capital punishment laws. The nine separate opinions were loaded with surveys, statistical studies and essays on legal history. The only thing they didn't contain were straightforward conclusions as to whether a cold-blooded killing by an individual constitutionally justified a cold-blooded killing by the state. The next year the justices issued opinions of epic lengths concluding that abortion should have some constitutional protection. Again, their work product was replete with expert analysis and informational detail that seemed oddly detached from their tentative conclusions. When the Court decided in 1980 that a life sentence for three petty offenses was not cruel and unusual punishment, it put on display an awesome array of information regarding the punishment practices of the 50 states which did little to validate its decision.

These informationally weighty decisions proved to have the life spans of the latest editions of computer software. Being founded on masses of specific information, they were vulnerable to later onslaughts by different information assembled to justify different points of view. By 1976, the death penalty had been reinstated; by 1983, life sentences for petty offenses had been deconstitutionalized; and abortion law is pulverized into new shapeless masses every few years.

We have to a large degree lost wisdom in knowledge, and knowledge in information, and the most disturbing part is, it all seems to be a natural human process. Our courts would probably reverse the trend if they could, but no one seems to know quite how to do it.

54.

ZOOLOGY AS LAW

"[I]f it be a beast that is <u>ferae naturae</u>, as a lion, a bear, a wolf, <u>yea, an ape or a monkey</u>, if he get loose and do harm to any person, the owner is liable to an action for the damage...." (Emphasis added).

Georgia Court of Appeals, 1936, quoting Lord Hale, early 17th Century.

On the morning of February 16, 1935, Mrs. M.L. Smith of DeKalb County, Georgia left her house to go shopping. As she approached her car she suddenly realized that "a large baboon, approximately the size of an Airedale dog" was sitting behind the wheel. When she halted in alarm, the baboon clamored out of the car and approached her "in a menacing manner". In her haste to return to the safety of her house, Mrs. Smith tripped over the front door mat and barked her shin. The baboon realized that he could accomplish nothing in that direction and returned to the car, where he leisurely destroyed the contents of Mrs. Smith's purse.

As might be imagined, the simian assault distressed the lady greatly. Memories of the bizarre threatening apparition haunted her thoughts and dreams for months. As is usual in such cases, she consulted her doctor first and then her lawyer.

The owner of the baboon turned out to be one Asa Candler who maintained a large private menagerie in the neighborhood. The baboon had escaped with the assistance of an elk, which was confined in a neighboring cage. The elk had torn a hole in an adjoining fence and the baboon had gone through it.

The jury returned a verdict in favor of Mrs. Smith for $10,000. On appeal, Candler's lawyer argued that there should have been no judgment because Candler had taken reasonable precautions to keep the baboon fenced in. He argued that his client should not be held responsible either for the complicity of the elk or the unexpected aggressiveness of the baboon.

On the face of it, the case appeared to present a unique and extraordinarily difficult issue. What principles of liability could possibly exist with respect to the maintenance of a baboon? When the judges went to the library, however, they discovered that English and American legal history was full of escaping animals, and that the rules of liability were generally clear. When an ordinary domestic animal such as a dog or a pig got loose, the owner was held responsible only if he had carelessly let it roam at large. Naturally fierce (*ferae naturae*) animals, such as tigers and cobras, were another matter. People who chose to keep such creatures did so at their peril. If they escaped, their owners were strictly liable for whatever injury they caused, regardless of how careful they had tried to be. The great question in the Candler case was whether a baboon should be classified as naturally docile like a pig, or naturally ferocious like a tiger.

The judges were relieved to find that the dusty archives of history provided a precise answer. Three centuries previously, Lord Hale had hit the nail directly on the head. His classification of apes and monkeys as *ferae naturae* sealed Asa Candler's financial fate—the $10,000 judgment would have to be paid.

Who says that law is an imprecise science?

55.

A GREAT LIBEL OF A GREAT JUSTICE

"The presence on the bench of a justice who has worn the white robe of the Ku Klux Klan will stand as a living symbol of the fact that here the cause of liberalism was unwittingly betrayed."

New York Times, 1937, criticizing the appointment of Justice Hugo Black.

The shame was that the *Times* knew better. No hater, Hugo Black had been a nominal member of the Klan from 1923 to 1925. Most Birmingham Alabama lawyers were members in those days. It was not much more of an ideological commitment than joining the Kiwanis Club might be. It was not an enlightened gesture, but neither was it the ugly underwriting of racial injustice it appeared to be from a distance of 14 years. If penance had been necessary, Black had long since done it. As a U.S. Senator, he had been an unapologetic liberal, one of the few Southern allies F.D.R. could count on in constructing his New Deal.

But when the story of the Klan connection broke, the *Times* found it too "good" to resist. Mindlessly joining a press "orgy of vituperation" it printed what it knew to be false: that Black's elevation to the Court was a "betrayal of liberalism".

It was, of course, nothing of the kind. Black was to become a fearless champion of racial justice during his long tenure on the Court, spearheading the drive to desegregate the South. He was repaid in the hard coin of enmity. When he returned home to Birmingham after the seminal school desegregation case, *Brown v. Board of Education*, was decided in 1954, his friends and constituents shunned and reviled him. When he entered the dining room of a local country club he was roundly booed, and he had to wear a chest protector provided by the Secret Service in his rare appearances on public streets. His old law school refused to invite him to its fiftieth reunion in 1956, and a state legislator introduced a bill to pay his funeral expenses, provided he was buried elsewhere than in Alabama.

In 1964, a great case involving Black's old nemesis the *Times*—*New York Times v. Sullivan*—came before the Court. The Court's decision gave the *Times*, and all other publications, sweeping new First Amendment protection. It held that a public official could not recover damages in a libel suit unless the publication had knowingly or recklessly published false facts about him. Justice Black was disappointed at the Court's timidity in protecting the rights of a free press. "I base my vote to reverse," he wrote,

> On the belief that the First and Fourteenth Amendments not only "delimit" a state's power to award damages to public officials against critics of their official conduct' but completely prohibit the state from exercising such a power ... An unconditional right to say what one pleases about public affairs is what I consider to be the minimum guarantee of the First Amendment.
> I regret that the Court has stopped short of this holding, indispensable to preserving our free press from destruction.

The "Betrayer of Liberalism" had not only voted to give the *Times* unlimited power to do to others what it had done to him, he had voted to absolve it of liability for publishing a false report regarding racial suppression in Alabama. He had shown more guts in confronting the moral cross-current of his time than any *New York Times* editorial writer ever dreamed of. If ever a man deserved a retraction, Hugo Black did. Of course, he neither got nor expected one. He knew that in law, as in life, virtue is its own reward, because it has to be.

56.

A CREATIVE DEFENSE TO A BRIBERY CHARGE BY A CROOKED JUDGE

"My decisions were impeccably correct—I dispensed nothing but justice."

Judge Martin Manton (1938).

Martin Manton bears a unique distinction. He is the only federal appeals judge in the history of the United States to be convicted of selling justice while on the Bench. He did an impressive job of setting that precedent. If crooked judges are artists, Manton was Michelangelo.

He "served" on the Second Circuit Court of Appeals from 1930 until his forced departure in 1938. The Second Circuit has been graced with such greats as Learned Hand and Jerome Frank, and has a well-earned reputation as the best appeals court in the country. Manton was as brilliant as most of his colleagues, but so, probably, was Judas Escariet.

He took thousands of dollars in bribes for writing "favorable" decisions. Federal appeals cases are decided by three judge panels, and Manton's brethren were honest. He therefore had to be careful to choose cases which could plausibly be decided in favor of his customers, and he usually chose cases in which he was the presiding judge. The most important requirements, of course, were that the case be financially significant and the parties well-heeled. To give him his due, he always delivered as promised, although on one occasion he did so by only a two to one vote.

When he was finally indicted and brought to trial on federal bribery charges he predictably denied everything. He asserted another defense, however, that had considerably more flare. He argued that he had done no wrong, because all of his decisions had been legally correct! His customers had bought only justice and who could complain about that? On the appeal of his conviction, his old court gave the argument short shrift. "There is nothing in the point", wrote Supreme Court Justice Sutherland, who had been specially appointed to participate in the appeal. "Judicial action, whether just or unjust, right or wrong, is not for sale."

57.

THE MOST DESPISED SUPREME COURT JUSTICE

"A savagely sarcastic, incredibly reactionary Puritan anti-Semite".

Time Magazine, describing Supreme Court Justice James Clark McReynolds, 1939.

The above quote is actually a routine example of the things that were said about Justice McReynolds. A 1936 *Fortune* magazine article labeled him a "flauntingly disagreeable character", a book published in the same year called him the Supreme Court's "greatest human tragedy", and another published in 1943 called him "the narrowest, rudest, laziest man on the Bench".

He earned these epithets. Those who knew McReynolds best liked him least. It was said that "few justices, perhaps none, ever found it possible to carry on harmoniously with him," and that "his demeanor on the Bench was a disgrace to the Court." Chief Justice William Taft, who was famous for being easy to get along with, described him this way: "He is inconsiderate of his colleagues and others, and contemptuous of everyone. A fine looking fellow, a man of real ability, he has been spoiled for usefulness."

McReynolds was a supermarket of petty hatreds. He vociferously despised red nail polish on women, wrist watches on men, rare meat, tobacco, having his portrait painted, whispering during Supreme Court arguments, improper protocol toward justices at social functions, flattery, dancing, athletics and "unAmericans".

As the *Time* article noted, anti-Semitism was a McReynolds specialty. His behavior toward the Jewish members of the Court was simply inexcusable. He refused to speak to Louis Brandeis for three years after he came on the Court because Brandeis was Jewish. For the same reason, he refused to travel with the Court to Philadelphia in 1922, explaining to Taft, "As you know, I am not always to be found where there is a Hebrew aboard." Taft canceled the Court picture in 1924 because McReynolds refused to sit next to Brandeis. When the great Jewish justice retired from the Court, a gracious letter of farewell was composed by his appreciative brethren. McReynolds would not sign it.

He immediately let Brandeis' Jewish successor, the gentle Benjamin Cardozo, know that he would receive the same treatment. During Cardozo's swearing in ceremony, McReynolds ostentatiously leaned back in his seat and read a newspaper.

The Court's reaction to McReynolds' own departure from the Bench has not been chronicled, but there can not have been a wet eye in the house.

58.

AN INSIGHTFUL LITERARY DESCRIPTION OF REAL JURY ATTITUDES

> "Justice for all was a principle [the jurors] understood and believed in; but by 'all' they did not perhaps really mean persons low-down and no good ... If [an accused person's] reputation and presence were good, he was presumed to be innocent; if they were bad, he was presumed to be guilty. If the law presumed differently, the law presumed alone."
>
> James Cozzens, *The Just and the Unjust*, 1942.

Like religion, law operates largely on hope. It knows that its standards are unrealistic as applied to imperfect mortals. No lawyer can refrain from coaching his clients a little. If there are two ways of phrasing a truthful statement, witnesses choose the one that favors the side they favor. Judges who claim to be free of bias have two vices—bias and dishonesty.

When James Cozzens compared what juries do with what they are supposed to do, he cut to the marrow of the American justice system. Here is the defendant, slouching at the counsel table, despite his lawyer's command to sit up straight. He has a record, and no visible supporting family in the courtroom. The offensive incoherence of his testimony is mitigated only by its stunning brevity. What did he say? Something about being in Atlanta when the murder was "did"? The jury is expected to receive this testimony, to the extent they can decipher it, with scientific indifference to its source.

Jurors are to leave their prejudices at the courtroom door—not only the racial ones, but prejudices against blatant stupidity, apparent meanness and the tendency to crack knuckles at the counsel table. They are expected, in short, to judge the offense and not the man accused of committing it. If he is on trial for robbery, and it is proven that he has robbed sixteen other banks, jurors are prohibited from following the obvious chain of reasoning every red-blooded—or for that matter blue-blooded—American would pursue: 1) the defendant is a bank robber; 2) he is therefore probably guilty of this particular robbery.

No jury is capable of forgetting that the defendant is an obnoxious, knuckle-cracking bank robber when it gets around to deciding his guilt, and few have any interest in trying. If the law presumes juries try offenses, not people, it does indeed "presume alone".

Of course, the law does not actually presume any such thing. It knows that judges, lawyers, witnesses and juries never achieve the standards imposed on them, but it believes that if they stretch to do so, justice will be served as well as it can be. In this, the precepts of the law do not differ greatly from the precepts of religion.

59.

FEAR SWALLOWS DUE PROCESS

> "[This] is an attempt to make an otherwise innocent act a crime merely because this prisoner is the son of parents as to whom he has no choice, and belongs to a race from which there is no way to resign."
>
> Justice Robert Jackson, dissenting in *United States v. Korematsu*, (1944).

Like marriage vows, the Bill of Rights guarantees are harder to keep when times get really tough. Benjamin Franklin warned that a people willing to sacrifice freedom for security would end up with neither. It's a lesson the Nation has never quite fully learned. Our greatest president, Abraham Lincoln, suspended the writ of *habeas corpus* in a non-military area during the civil war; the Supreme Court rebuked him for doing so after his life and the war had ended. Oliver Wendell Holmes wrote that we must allow freedom for the expression of ideas "we hate and believe to be fraught with death" in a brilliant dissenting opinion; the majority opinion affirmed the twenty year sentence of a little man because he had thrown harmless pro-Bolshevik leaflets from a rooftop. When FDR proclaimed that "the only thing we have to fear is fear itself," he was talking about the Depression, but the statement applies with even greater force to the preservation of our basic liberties. Fear is their great enemy and destroyer.

* * * *

In 1942 a Californian named Fred celebrated his twenty-third birthday. He wanted to help his country but was restricted in his ability to do so. In 1941 he had tried to enlist in the Army but had been rejected because of a stomach ulcer. The next best thing he could do was to aid the war effort in a civilian capacity, which he did. He became a welder in a California shipyard which was constructing ships for the Navy's wartime fleet.

His girlfriend was an Italian named Ida Boitano, whom he hoped one day to marry. It was the Great American Story, except for one fatal fact. Fred's last name was Korematsu and his parents had been born in Japan. Fred himself knew almost no Japanese and had never been to Japan, or, indeed, any other foreign country. He was as American as apple pie—or, perhaps chop suey.

Unknown to Fred Korematsu, President Franklin Roosevelt—for whom Fred had enthusiastically voted—entered an order in November, 1941 requiring that the names and addresses of all American Japanese persons be compiled. After Pearl Harbor on December 7, 1941, America had reasons to fear the direct application of Japanese military power. The Japanese had shelled Santa Barbara, California and Seaside, Oregon and a Japanese submarine had sunk a ship near Seattle, Washington. These actions kindled public hysteria, including fears of Japanese sabotage, and as usual, American citizens demanded a "solution".

The solution in this case was shameful. On February 19, 1942, President Roosevelt signed Executive Order 9066 establishing "prescribed military areas … from which any and all persons may be excluded (i.e., those of Japanese ancestry)". Concentration camps would be set up in a so-called Zone of the Interior into which such "persons" would be herded. The victims were characteristically given one week to vacate their West Coast homes, which forced them to conduct what amounted to confiscatory yard sales, in which their personal property was sold at a fraction of its value. They were first "housed" in makeshift "assembly centers", some of which were horse stables stinking from manure, and then sent to crude desert housing to live under broiling suns with nothing to do but wait for eventual release.

Fred Korematsu resolved to escape the camps by moving to Nevada, but when the deadline for evacuation of May 7, 1942 arrived, he was not economically or otherwise prepared to flee. On May 30, 1942 he resolved to test the constitutionality of the evacuation order by turning himself in to the San Leandro police department. Surely, the order was unconstitutional as applied to American-born citizens, regardless of the color of their skin or the source of their ancestry. Fred's girlfriend, for example, was of Italian extraction, and Italy as well as Japan was a wartime enemy of America. Why him and not her?

Fred's case ultimately found its way to the United States Supreme Court where, to its everlasting shame, the Court affirmed his conviction.

In a dissenting opinion, Justice Robert Jackson summed up the case in excruciatingly plain English:

> Korematsu was born on our soil, of parents born in Japan. The constitution makes him a citizen of the United States by nativity and a citizen of California by residence. No claim is made that he is not loyal to this Country …

> Korematsu, however, has been convicted of an act not commonly a crime. It consists of being merely present in the state whereof he is a citizen, near the place where he was born, and where all his life he has lived.

Jackson pointed out that under the American Constitution "guilt is personal and not inheritable". He noted that even if Korematsu's parents had been convicted traitors, instead of natives of Japan, their guilt could not have been visited upon their son. The Constitution, he wrote, "provides that 'no Attainder of Treason shall work Corruption of Blood or Forfeiture except during the Life of the Person attainted'".

> But here is an attempt to make an otherwise innocent act a crime merely because this prisoner is the son of parents as to whom he has no choice, and belongs to a race from which there is no way to resign.

The true impetus for the majority decision was revealed in a short passage toward the end of the "reasoning" portion of the opinion. "[W]e are not unmindful of the hardships imposed ... upon a large group of Americans. But hardships are part of war and war is an aggregation of hardship. All citizens alike, both in and out of uniform, feel the impact of war in greater or lesser measures." This theme appeared in every walk of life during World War II. Many hundreds of thousands of young men were facing the threat and reality of death in combat for the protection of their Country's interests. By comparison, every lesser sacrifice by other citizens tended to be held for little or naught. Compassion and fairness to an extent took a vacation during the War, as it seems to during all wars. Even if innocent of wrong-doing, how could Korematsu legitimately complain about the discomfort of a little residential relocation? At least he wasn't in a foxhole[5].

It is said that truth is the first casualty of war. Decency is a close competitor.

---

5   Neither were the more racially and economically advantaged businessmen of America, who stoutly resisted an excess profits tax intended to aid the war effort. If you are going to try to go to war ... in a capitalist country, you have got to let business make money out of the process, or businessmen won't work, explained Secretary of War Edward Stinson in a 1940 letter. Home front patriotic sacrifice was, shall we say, rather selectively exacted.

60.

UNMASKING ROBIN HOOD

"Right merrily they dwelt within the depths of Sherwood Forest, suffering neither care nor want, but passing time in merry games of archery or bouts of cudgel play; living upon the King's venison, Robin himself, but all the band were outlaws and dwelled apart from other men, yet they were loved by the country people round about."

Howard Pyle, 1946.

America's romantic view of English outlawry is based on lyrical portraits such as this. It is the Robin Hood we all grew up with. Unfortunately, it is also a gigantic fraud. Pyle's famous passage describes the life of the English outlaw about as accurately as "Leave It To Beaver" described the life of an inter-city ghetto family. Real English outlaws were nothing like the fabled merry men of American storybooks and movies. Far from being happy, carefree and loved, they were miserable, hunted and despised. Far from being distinctive political exiles, they were a vast heard of common murderers, rapists and other thugs who roamed the bogs and forests of England, hiding from the hangmen and pillaging for survival. If the real Robin Hood felt any merriment, it was probably from all of that October ale he swilled—and God knows where he got it.

Real outlaws had the status of dangerous wild animals. It was "the right of every man to pursue [an outlaw], to ravage his land, to burn his house, to hunt him down like a wild beast and slay him for a wild beast he [was]." The law was not satisfied with marking outlaws for death, it made them non-people in every way. When a man was declared an outlaw, every legal relationship he had was forever dissolved. He had no contract rights, he had no marriage, no one owed him homage, his personal property was forfeited to the King, and the King could lay waste to his land and seize it. His blood was "corrupted", which meant that his children could never inherit, not only from him, but from anyone.

The modern Robin Hood story, prettified though it is, is rooted in this miserable reality. Among the herd of murderous thugs and desperate fugitives, there was a small elite of high-class outlaws who captured the public's imagination. They operated in organized gangs, moving, as one 14th Century indictment put it, "in manner of war", murdering and kidnapping the mighty, freeing captured allies, and in general behaving like underground governments. These elitists were models for the earliest Robin Hood tales.

When we read these ancient tales, however, we see a dark and unfamiliar Robin. He has the skill and daring of Pyle's hero, but not his humanity. When he and his men rob the rich, they pocket the proceeds instead of giving them to the poor. They do not fight for the King, but to survive and profit. Above all, they are starkly violent men. They do not merely knock people on the head and capture them, or humiliate them at a forest feast. They kill them in cold blood and, with chilling consistency, cut off their heads. In one of the oldest surviving tales, Robin beheads Guy of Gisborne and carries his mangled head around the neighborhood on the end of his bow. He also needlessly beheads the Sheriff after shooting him dead. His henchman, Much the Miller's son, lopes off the head of a young page just to keep him quiet. It is all done without emotion, in the manner of practiced murderers.

Hark the distant laughter! It is Robin and his merry men, roasting their dinner and drinking to their guests? No! It is Robyn and his beery men, drinking their dinner and roasting their guests.

61.

THE BEST USE OF SHAKESPEARE IN A FINAL ARGUMENT

"[The Nazi defendants] stand before the record of this trial as blood-stained Gloucester stood by the body of his slain King. He begged of the widow, as they beg of you: "Say I slew them not." And the Queen replied, "Then say they were not slain. But dead they are ... "If you were to say of these men that they are not guilty, it would be as true to say that there has been no war, there are no slain, there has been no crime."

Chief Prosecutor Robert Jackson, closing the Allies' case at the Nuremburg war crimes trial, 1946.

Even the finest courtroom arguments tend to have disappointing endings. Anxiety over the verdict causes the advocate to end by admonishing the judge or jury, in workaday words, simply to do their duty. Jackson's concluding peroration at Nuremburg stands as a mighty exception to that rule.

The Nuremburg prosecutions were a exceptional lawyer's dream come true. They were truly the trials of the century, perhaps of the millennium. Opinions about their legitimacy were fiercely divided. Some jurists thought they violated constitutional principles, because they punished the defendants for conduct—such as "the waging of aggressive warfare"—that had not been defined as a crime at the time it was committed. Others thought they were a vital landmark on humankind's journey up from savagery, because they applied the rule of law to the conduct of nations. However they were viewed, they were momentous. Lawyers rarely encounter a judicial event big enough to accommodate eloquence on a truly grand scale, but Nuremburg uniquely did so.

The brilliant Robert Jackson made the most of his rhetorical opportunity. He told the judges that "the terror of Torquemada pales before the Nazi Inquest", that the principal defendants were culpable "as Hitler's Praetorean Guard" who, although "they were under Caesar's orders, Caesar was always in their hands", and that the immensity of the crimes he was reviewing forced him "as Kipling put it, [to] splash at a 10-league canvas with brushes of comet's hair".

Reporter Rebecca West called his argument "patently admirable, patently a pattern of the material necessary to the salvation of people". Then she wrote something that the passage of more than half a century has cast in doubt. Commenting on the final argument of British prosecutor Sir Hartley Shawcross, she called it "not so shapely and so decorative as Mr. Justice Jackson's, for English rhetoric has crossed the Atlantic in this century and is now more at home in the United States than on its native ground...." Those who have observed the latest offerings of the American Bar in televised criminal trials or read recent Supreme Court opinions may consider this compliment premature.

As is true of all memorable prosecution arguments, the greatness of Jackson's speech reflected the greatness of the wrongs he condemned. If the Nazis' crimes had lacked their special horror, Jackson's rhetorical *tour de force* might have sounded like inspired vaudeville. From this standpoint, it might be better for us all if Shakespeare is never again quoted in a final argument.

62.

AN ELOQUENT MOMENT IN THE HISTORY OF CAPITAL PUNISHMENT

"You feel like you got a mouth full of cold peanut butter and you see little blue and pink and green speckles in front of your eyes, the kind that shines in a rooster's tail ..."

Willie Francis, 1947.

An American horror story was played out in the mid-1940's, when the state of Louisiana sent a black teenager named Willie Francis to his death—twice.

Francis was convicted of murder by a Louisiana jury and sentenced to death. On May 3, 1946, he was taken to the death room in the state penitentiary and strapped into the electric chair. The sheriff asked him if he wanted to say anything, but he did not respond. A black hood was placed over his head. The executioner adjusted the mechanism which activated the current and when the needle on the dial reached the appropriate point he pulled the switch down, saying "Goodbye Willie." According to the attending chaplain "the condemned man's lips puffed out and his body squirmed and tensed and he jumped so that the chair rocked on the floor." But he did not die. "Take it off. Let me breathe," Willie Francis gasped. The executioner turned off the switch and lifted the hood, revealing the condemned boy's stricken face. A few minutes later the sheriff entered the room and announced that the governor had granted a reprieve.

Francis gave an unforgettable account of his near approach to death to a reporter for the *New York Herald Tribune*: "You feel like you got a mouth full of cold peanut butter and you see little blue and pink and green speckles in front of your eyes, the kind that shines in a rooster's tail," he said. "All I could think of was, Willie, you're going out'n this world." He went on to describe the terror of imminent death in dark and primitive poetry: "They begun to strap me against the chair and everything begun to look dazy in the room. It was like the white folks was watching on a big swing and they swung away-y-y back and then right up close to me where I could hear their breathing. I didn't think of my whole life like at the picture show, just Willie, you're going out'n this world in this bad chair. Sometimes I thought it so loud it hurt my head and when they put the black bag over my head I was all locked up inside the bag with the loud thinking." He described the color of death: "Some folks say its gold; some say its white as hominy grits; I reckon its black. I ought to know, I been mighty close." He said that when the "electric man" said "goodbye" to him, he was too frightened to answer. "He could have been puttin' me on a bus to New Orleans the way he said it. I tried to say goodbye but my tongue got stuck in the peanut butter ..."

When the case was argued before the Supreme Court on November 18, 1946, Francis' lawyer did everything within his power to convey its unique horror to the justices, insisting that a second application of the electric chair to Willie would violate the Eighth Amendment's prohibition against cruel and unusual punishments. The argument was strong enough to convince four of the justices that the case should be remanded to the trial court to make findings regarding the physical cruelty of the aborted execution. It was too weak to convince the other four, however, and the 4-4 tie meant that Willie Francis must die. When Francis saw the Court's opinion, the word "affirmed" must have come at him as "dazily" as the white folks on the swing.

The *Francis* case help spark a movement to abolish the death penalty which radically changed the standards for inflicting it over the next several decades. That movement has had some powerful spokesmen, but none capable of matching the soft-spoken eloquence of the 15-year-old Louisiana boy who looked state-sponsored death in the face, and lived to tell the rest of us what it looked like.

63.

A SMALL TESTIMONIAL FUSE LIGHTS A HUGE POLITICAL EXPLOSION

> Counsel: "Have you ever seen a Prothonotary Warbler?"
> Hiss: "Yes, I have. Right _here_ on the Potomac."
>
> Alger Hiss, testifying before the House UnAmerican Activities Committee, 1948.

When Whitaker Chambers shambled into the House UnAmerican Activities Committee room on August 3, 1948, and told his bizarre tale, the members didn't think it would come to much. Chambers was what authors call "unprepossessing". Physically ponderous, homely and a sloppy dresser, he was not the type to stimulate allegiance from the Establishment. His accusations were, if anything, even less palatable to the Committee members than his appearance. He told them that Alger Hiss, one of the brightest stars in the American public firmament, had been—might still be—an active member of the Communist Party. Hiss was then chairman of the Carnegie Endowment Fund. He had been a brilliant Harvard law student, a clerk to Justice Felix Frankfurter, a high-ranking state department official and, in general, a notable asset to the liberal side of the American way of life. Many of the Committee members had political reasons for wanting to believe Chambers, but his charges seemed too fantastic to be true and too risky to accept.

Chambers had admittedly been a member of the Party himself, from 1925 to 1938 and an editor of the Communist newspaper, _The Daily Worker_. He testified that when he quit the Party he had begged his friend Alger to quit too, but Alger had declined. He and Alger had cried, he said. "You _cried_?" repeated the Committee counsel. "We cried," Chambers assured him.

In the midst of his random ruminations, Chambers happened to mention that Hiss and his wife were avid bird watchers. One day Hiss had excitedly told Chambers that he had seen a Prothonotary Warbler during an early morning stroll, Chambers said. The Committee counsel nodded absently, and soon afterwards dismissed Chambers from the witness chair.

In his own appearance before the Committee, Hiss was as crisp and impressive as Chambers had been slovenly and disreputable. He convincingly denied ever knowing a Whitaker Chambers. The Committee members seemed prepared to believe him; most of them, in fact, seemed embarrassed that the question had been asked. Then an errant thought struck the Committee counsel. "Have you ever seen a Prothonotary Warbler?", he impulsively asked. "Yes, I have," Hiss replied enthusiastically. "Right <u>here</u>, on the Potomac." So much for not knowing Whitaker Chambers.

The credibility compass had swung 180 degrees. The Republican majority on the Committee, led by a hyper-ambitious young Congressman named Richard Nixon, suddenly detected the odor of blood in the political water. A dramatic confrontation was arranged between Chambers and Hiss at a local hotel, after which Hiss was forced to admit he had known Chambers "under another name". Within a year Hiss had been indicted for committing perjury in his testimony before the Committee. After one mistrial, he was convicted in a second trial and sentenced to the penitentiary.

His conviction launched Richard Nixon as a major political figure, and made possible all of the nation-shaking events produced by that remarkable career. It also helped launch the so-called McCarthy Era, which would torment America for a decade and alter its political direction for many more.

* * * *

There is an 18th Century short story about a party of Englishmen who traveled back through time. Their journey was closely supervised, so as to avoid disturbing the ecology whose chronological laws they were violating. The travelers were ordered to stay on a suspended walkway, and not to have any contact with the environment they were visiting. One disobeyed and accidently killed a butterfly. When they returned to the 18th Century, they discovered an alien and terrible world, utterly altered by that butterfly's death, eons ago.

Hiss' Prothonotary Warbler may well be a modest modern version of that fictional butterfly. If Whitaker Chambers had been a little less gregarious, if he had omitted that seemingly innocent little bird from his testimony, 1950's America might have been quite different. There were, of course, innumerable other ways in which Hiss might have been exposed, and the McCarthy Era might have been inevitable, with or without the Hiss conviction. Still, there is only one way to judge history with certainty, and that is by what actually happened. By that test, Hiss' little Warbler looms immeasurably large.

64.

A DEPRESSINGLY "REALISTIC" VIEW OF THE AMERICAN TRIAL PROCESS

"Our present trial method is … the equivalent of throwing pepper in the eyes of a surgeon when he is performing an operation."

Federal Court of Appeals Judge Jerome Frank, 1949.

Judge Frank was brilliant, to the point of eccentricity. He was a leader of the so-called Realist school of jurisprudence, which believed in calling a legal spade a spade. Lawyers and judges tend to describe the law in unreal terms—as it should be, has been said to be, or as they wish it to be—rather than as it is. Frank and his comrades specialized in tearing the pretty masks off the faces of the law. What they exposed was not always uplifting or dignifying, but in its own way, it was more interesting than the traditional cant.

The above quote is taken from Frank's intriguing book Courts on Trial. It appeared in a chapter called the "Fight Theory Versus the Truth Theory". Other chapters were headed "The Needless Mystery of Courthouse Government", "Facts are Guesses", "Modern Legal Magic", "The Upper Court Myth" and "The Cult of the Robe".

The "pepper in the surgeon's eyes" comment stated an important reality. The traditional view is that trials are searches for truth, analogous to what goes on in a laboratory. Contending parties, motivated by competing self-interest, present every conceivable fact and argument. The adjudicating body (a jury) is selected by the parties to be as objective as possible. Rules of evidence cull out irrelevant and unduly inflammatory facts. A presiding judge insures that everyone concerned follows principles of decision-making validated by years of practical experience. The American trial process, it is said, is the best truth-finding mechanism yet devised by mankind for resolving disputes.

If so, mankind is in serious trouble. As a truth-finder, the typical trial is better than palm reading, but considerably worse than an eye examination.

The fact is that the purpose of a trial is not necessarily to establish truth, but to resolve disputes—truth being a welcome, but non-essential, by-product. Unlike a scientific report, a verdict is not conclusive because it is right, it is right because it is conclusive. A baseball umpire once described a similar American decision-making process this way: "Some pitches are strikes, and some pitches are balls, but they ain't nothing until I call them."

The true analogy for the trial is not a scientific investigation, but a fight. The historical antecedent of jury trial was trial by battle, to the death if necessary. The aim of the modern lawyer is not—cannot be—an objective uncovering of facts. It is victory for his client. Trial practice handbooks advise lawyers to question opposing witnesses carefully, so that no unexpectedly revealing information will be provided, to "destroy the effect of an adverse witness by making him appear more hostile than he really is", or to "tempt the witness to indulge in his propensity for exaggeration, so as to make him hang himself". It is a process designed to reveal truth in about the same sense that a poker game is.

Ask any client who has been through a trial whether it <u>seemed</u> like an investigation of the truth. He will probably tell you that it seemed like nothing he had every experienced before, and that he hardly recognized the facts of his own case in the flow of verbal combat. "If you lead your client into the courtroom with you," Judge Learned Hand once told a lawyer, "you will, if you have the nerve to watch him, see in his face a baffled sense that there is going on, some kind of game, which, while its outcome may be tragic to him, is incomprehensible."

Of course, trials usually do produce results that are acceptable as "truth"— the common sense of juries is capable of overcoming the best efforts to defeat it. Despite the discomfort of the pepper, the operation usually turns out to be more or less successful. The general rightness of jury verdicts is, in fact, one of the natural miracles of our civilization.

65.

AN ILL-ADVISED LITERARY FLOURISH

"These cases are remanded to the District Courts to take such proceedings and enter such orders and decrees consistent with this opinion as are necessary in order to admit to public schools on a racially non-discriminatory basis with all deliberate speed the parties to these cases." (Emphasis added).

Brown v. Board of Education, (1955).

In the Supreme Court's two hundred year history, no words have come back to haunt it more relentlessly than the odd little phrase "with all deliberate speed." Chief Justice Warren must have wished a thousand times that he could erase those words from the Brown opinion. They were written to allow limited flexibility in scheduling school desegregation, but for fifteen years after they appeared, school boards used them as an excuse for doing nothing and doing it exceedingly slowly.

Warren was a blunt word-smith who usually managed to say what he meant with clarity, if not necessarily with grace. He was talked into using the unusual, counter-productive phrase by the intellectual Justice Frankfurter, who later revealed that it had a high-class intellectual lineage. Its oldest documented use was by British poet Francis Thompson in an 1893 poem, "The Hound of Heaven". Justice Oliver Wendell Holmes referred to it in a 1909 letter to Sir Frederick Pollock, calling it "a delightful phrase", and later used it in one of his Supreme Court opinions. Frankfurter told Warren that it was the perfect language for ordering desegregation, and the new Chief Justice—perhaps intimidated by Frankfurter's more experienced and supposedly superior judicial intellect—unwisely bought the suggestion.

In 1969, the Supreme Court finally jammed the verbal genie back into the bottle, ruling that deliberate speed in school desegregation cases was "no longer constitutionally permissible." This was, to many, a truly "delightful phrase", despite its lack of literary quality.

66.

GIVE ME LIBERTY OR GIVE ME—SOMETHING

"I'd rather have a little of my liberty chipped away today than have it all taken away tomorrow."

Supreme Court Justice Sherman Minton, 1956.

The closer one gets to viewing the apex of judicial power in America, the more nervous one becomes. Such nervousness arises from two facts: 1) the ultimate constitutional, and therefore political, power in this country is wielded by nine people—or, more precisely, by the one to three people who represent the usual margin of decision in Supreme Court opinions, and 2) while a few of these people have been brilliant and noble, most of them have been merely competent, and some have been terrifyingly mediocre.

Sherman Minton, appointed in the early 1950's by President Truman, resided in the third category. A charitable assessment acknowledges that he "was never an intellectual giant", a poll of history scholars places him among the eight worst justices of all time, and a recent Supreme Court biography states that "by any standard he ranks near the bottom of any list of justices".

He made the statement quoted above during an historic Supreme Court conference. The Court was discussing a group of communist sedition cases, in which individuals had been convicted and jailed for expressing views the authorities felt endangered the American form of government and way of life. It was these cases, more than anything else, that converted the previously moderate Earl Warren into the activist Chief Justice who led the Court on a constitutional revolution over the next 13 years of his tenure. They brought the conservative judicial restraint philosophy of Felix Frankfurter into direct collision with the free speech absolutism of Hugo Black, and the Court discussions of them were intellectually vigorous and often personally bitter. Minton's pusillanimous comment must have stunned his colleagues, and made Frankfurter wish for better allies.

But abject though it was, Minton's statement probably reflected the attitude of the average American. Most people would rather live in comfort than risk their security to enhance civil liberty—which is why our Bill of Rights principles are constantly in danger of being "chipped away".

67.

THE SUPREME COURT'S GREAT PHILOSOPHICAL DIVIDE

"Be a judge, Goddammit, be a judge."

Justice Felix Frankfurter to Chief Justice Earl Warren, circa 1959.

Frankfurter's angry admonition caught the essence of the most crucial constitutional conflict of our time: judicial restraint versus judicial activism. Frankfurter believed that judges must decide cases within an impersonal framework of principle called the Law. For him, personal opinion had no place in judging. Warren had come to the Court several years earlier with similar views, but by 1959 he had migrated to the activist position that would mark his work and the work of the Court for the remainder of his tenure. He had come to think that personal beliefs are not only a permissible, but a necessary, element of judicial decision-making. Better that a judge draw upon his own experience and moral viewpoints, he thought, than borrow the morality and experience of other judges, embalmed in case precedents.

Frankfurter's judicial restraint philosophy had led him to support mandatory flag salute laws that violated the religious beliefs of minorities, although he himself was a member of a religious minority; and to vote as a judge to uphold the cruel second execution of a black Louisiana teenager named Willie Francis, when the first attempt had failed, but he later worked as a private citizen to have the sentence commuted. When he told Warren to "be a judge" he was in some sense telling him: "Forget that you are a man." Warren's unwillingness to do so would eventually bring about changes in American law and life more profound than the two great antagonists could ever have predicted.

68.

AN ANTIQUATED RULE MEETS ITS LONG OVERDUE FATE

"The majority dogmatically announces that what has been the law of Pennsylvania, and what was the law going back to the Fogs and Mists of the formation of our common law, shall now be the law no longer!"

Pennsylvania Supreme Court Justice Michael Mussmano, 1960.

On September 21, 1958, Roy Ladd got into a "fight" with his girlfriend Dorothy Pearce, and beat her savagely. She died from complications on November 1, 1959. A murder indictment was obtained against Ladd by the Philadelphia District Attorney. The prosecutor undoubtedly knew that it would be a medically difficult case to prove, but he might not have known that it was an impossible case under existing law. Because of a seldom used thousand year old rule, Roy Ladd was innocent of murder regardless of what the evidence showed.

The so-called "Year and a Day Rule" said this: If a person strikes, stabs, stomps, poisons or otherwise physically afflicts another, and the victim dies more than a year and a day after the injury, no homicide has occurred. It is not just that prosecution is prevented—there is legally no killing. If the assailant can feed his victim enough chicken soup to get him or her past the three hundred and sixty-sixth day, he is an innocent man.

The Rule's origins are too remote to be traced, but it was already old when it appeared in a statute in 1278. There was a time when it made sense. The inefficiency of medieval weapons and the primitive quality of medical care combined to create long and dangerous convalescences for people wounded by criminal assaults. When death finally came, it was usually difficult to tell who or what was at fault: the original injury, whatever diseases may have intervened, the treatment of the wound itself.

Although medical science had long since become capable of determining the cause of death in most cases, and the Rule had long been denounced as an irrational anachronism, it had somehow survived into the 20th Century. American courts had continued to apply it as late as the 1940's.

The trial judge in Ladd's case refused to do so, however. He denied Ladd's motion to dismiss the indictment, and an appeal was taken to the Pennsylvania Supreme Court. The Court decided that it was time for the lumbering common law to catch up with common sense, and formally abolished the Rule. In noting that the medical rationale for the Rule had long since vanished, the Court said: "Where once there was darkness there is now light."

In his dissenting opinion, Judge Mussmano angrily begged to disagree. It is not unusual for judges to adhere to old legal concepts, but what made Mussmano's dissent in the <u>Ladd</u> case unusual was: 1) the utter irrelevance to contemporary life of the rule he argued for, and 2) his bitter vehemence in arguing for it. Not only did he thunder about the "Mists and Fogs of the Foundations of … the Common Law", he painted silly, lurid pictures of the horrors the decision would produce—assailants waiting "20, 30 or more years" to be prosecuted while their victims clung to life; crooked medical testimony "establishing" that "a slap in the face was the cause of a death fifteen years later." If he had been anything other than a judge, he would have been fired for writing nonsense.

There are logical reasons for illogical opinions like this. Some judges feel a scholarly connection with the past; they like old legal rules <u>because</u> they are old. Judges also tend to like power, and judicial power is at its greatest when it makes no common sense. A judge applying archaic law is like a witch doctor chanting magic incantations, while the ignorant masses watch in awe. Authority that is not understood is the purest form of power.

69.

THE ONLY JUSTICE KNOWN TO HAVE DISSENTED FROM HIS OWN MAJORITY OPINION

"The [insurance] policy here involved constituted only one property...."

Majority opinion in *Meyer v. United States*, written by Justice William Douglas, 1960.

"The government contends that ... the entire insurance proceeds of each policy are a single property ... and the Court so holds. Yet, with all deference, the conclusion is wide of the mark."

Dissenting opinion in *Meyer v. United States*, written by Justice William Douglas, 1960.

Actually, Douglas did not take credit for the majority opinion. He wrote it, but it was signed by Justice Charles Whitaker. Whitaker was perhaps the least competent Supreme Court Justice ever. He attended an unaccredited night law school, had a successful Kansas City law practice, was appointed to the Eighth Circuit Court of Appeals because of political connections, and was placed on the Supreme Court by President Eisenhower, who was presumably seeking the common touch. Whatever the reason for the appointment, the new Justice was clearly out of his depth. One of the justices reported that Whitaker once left a Court conference shaking his head and saying, "Felix [Frankfurter] used words in there I'd never heard of".

Whitaker's greatest weaknesses as a justice were his inability to come to a decision, and his incapacity to reduce it to writing after he had done so. These failings tended to intertwine. He would begin an opinion with one state of mind and the very act of writing would produce doubts and reversals in his thinking. He sometimes actually wept in frustration at the impossibility of the task. He finally had a nervous breakdown and retired from the Court in 1962, claiming permanent disability.

Justice William Douglas was at the other end of the competence spectrum. He dashed off opinions with what some regarded as too <u>much</u> facility and ease. He was perhaps the only justice in the history of the Court to complain that his work load was inadequate to occupy his time. He spent about half of his waking hours on his judicial labors, and the other half writing books, giving speeches, and enjoying the great outdoors and the company of women.

Meyer v. United States was a nondescript little case, involving the deductibility of Seven Thousand Dollars ($7,000) worth of insurance proceeds from an estate tax return. The issue was not complex, but it was intellectually tricky. Whitaker was appointed to write the majority opinion on behalf of six members of the Court, and Douglas wrote a three judge dissent. A few weeks after he had been given his assignment, Whitaker spoke to Douglas in desperation. "I can't seem to write this damn Meyer opinion," he said.

"That's because you're on the wrong side," Douglas replied.

"Not at all. Not at all," Whitaker said, "I'm right, but I can't get started."

"Would you like me to send you a draft of a majority opinion?" Douglas helpfully suggested.

"Would you please," Whitaker replied.

Within an hour, Douglas had written a majority opinion. He delivered it to Whitaker, who gratefully adopted it as his own.

And there they sit in Volume 364 of the *United States Reports*: two adroitly phrased, diametrically opposed opinions, in which Justice William Douglas vigorously disagreed with Justice William Douglas.

70.

HUGO IN WONDERLAND

"The beginning of the First Amendment is that 'Congress shall make no law' [abridging freedom of speech and press]. I understand that it is rather old-fashioned, and shows a slight naivete to say that 'no law' means no law. It is one of the most amazing things about the ingeniousness of the times that strong arguments are made, which <u>almost</u> convince me, that it is very foolish of me to think 'no law' means no law. But what it <u>says</u> is 'Congress shall make no law....'"

Justice Hugo Black, (circa 1964).

This powerfully simple formulation carried Justice Black through many a decisional storm. It was not as simple as it sounded, however. For example, "no law" may have meant no law, but what did "speech" mean? Late in his career, Black voted to uphold the expulsion of a student who had worn a t-shirt with a formidable four-letter word stenciled on the back. He obviously seemed to be violating his literal interpretation of the First Amendment. "Not at all", he explained. "Displaying <u>that</u> word is not speech, it's <u>conduct</u>."

* * * *

"You should say what you mean," the March Hare went on.
"I do," Alice hastily replied, "at least I mean what I say—that's the same thing, you know."

71.

A MOMENTOUS APOLOGY

"Judge I just wanted you to know that you were right and we were wrong."

Sam Englehart to Frank Johnson (late 1960's).

On February 1, 1956, the case of *Browder v. Gayle* was filed in the Federal District Court for the Middle District of Alabama, less than three months after Frank Johnson became the District Judge. Johnson was a man of extraordinary integrity. Although he was raised in segregated Alabama he had a profound allegiance to the Constitution and to simple fairness. More than any other judge of the time he used the law to make the civil rights movement a success. The grand principles were declared in far-off Washington but they had to be implemented case by case in southern court rooms, where the rubber of idealism met the rocky road of racial hatred. Johnson performed this operation nobly by simple adherence to his duty as a judge.

Mrs. Browder had been required to stand up on a Montgomery, Alabama bus to let a white person take her seat and had brought an action to enjoin enforcement of Montgomery's segregation laws. The case was heard by a three judge court, which included Johnson. As the junior judge, he spoke first during the Court's deliberations. His statement was characteristically simple and to the point: "State imposed segregation on public facilities violates the Constitution," he said. The Court's two to one decision in favor of the plaintiffs was later affirmed by the United States Supreme Court. Johnson said, "my vote ... was not based on any personal feeling that segregation was wrong; it was based on the law ... It wasn't for a judge to decide on the morality, but rather the law".

On May 4, 1961, a group of Freedom Riders inaugurated a bloody effort to integrate interstate buses. When they arrived at the Greyhound terminal in Montgomery, two hundred white people went on a rampage. Eventually the crowd swelled to 1,000. John Doar of the Justice Department prepared a petition for a federal injunction. A hearing was held on May 29th in Judge Johnson's court to enjoin the Ku Klux Klan, the Montgomery Police Department and numerous individuals from violating and failing to enforce the law.

Judge Johnson's order recited that the Montgomery Police Department knew the bus was coming, but had done nothing to prevent the violence that ensued.

> The failure of the Defendant law enforcement officers to enforce the law in this case clearly amounts to unlawful state action in violation of the Equal Protection Clause of the Fourteenth Amendment ... It [also] deprived the passengers of their rights without due process of law.

In March of 1965, Selma, Alabama law enforcement officers broke up—quite literally—a peaceful march conducted in protest of discriminatory voter registration. Terrific violence was inflicted on the marchers by Sheriff Jim Clark, his deputies and some auxiliary deputies known as "posse men".

The protestors subsequently planned to march 300 people, two abreast, along the left side of the highway between Selma and Montgomery, as a further protest of discriminatory registration and also of the violence that had occurred in Selma. Judge Johnson found that the "proposed plan to march from Selma to Montgomery, Alabama for its intended purposes is clearly a reasonable exercise of a right guaranteed by the Constitution of the United States" and that the plaintiffs were entitled to police protection on the march. The authorities were enjoined from "arresting, harassing, thwarting or in any way interfering with the effort to march from Selma to Montgomery".

"I didn't like demonstrations," Johnson later said, "even though I understood the reasons Blacks felt they needed to employ them. I feel now, and certainly felt during the civil rights movement in the South, that there is no place for anything that stirs up trouble or strife. All the boycotts, and sit-ins and marches in themselves did not cure the illness of discrimination. It was the court decisions that did it."

Years after the acid bitterness of Montgomery, Birmingham and Selma had passed into history Johnson was approached on a Montgomery street by a man named Sam Englehart. Englehart had been, in Johnson's words, "a big man in the White Citizens' Council," and one of Johnson's "strongest critics". He had served in the administration of segregationist Governor John Patterson during the early 1960's, and had been an outspoken advocate of its policies. Englehart called out to Johnson: "Hey, Judge. Judge Johnson, sir." Johnson stopped and waited. "Judge, I just wanted you to know that you were right, and we were wrong." Johnson stared at him. "I appreciate that," he said. Sam nodded and said, "Well, I didn't want to die without telling you that, Judge."

Frank Johnson always kept his feelings private, but there cannot have been many better moments in his life than that one. The desegregation decisions were physically enforced by literal armies of troops. But their impact on history is best measured by the quiet revolution in human hearts they ultimately caused.

72.

HOPPING ABOARD PRESIDENT KENNEDY'S HEARSE

"You sit here in judgment of Clay Shaw."

New Orleans District Attorney Jim Garrison (1969).

America has known many prosecutors who used their power to gain glory, but there was no real precedent for Jim Garrison. From the day he became New Orleans District Attorney, he used his office as a ticket to national fame with a shameless single-mindedness. The Clay Shaw prosecution was merely the most spectacular in a series of capers, in which Garrison converted public service into private opportunity.

If he had an American analog, it was Senator Joseph McCarthy. Such men look for, not what is true, but what is "hot". In McCarthy's 1950's, it was communism. In Garrison's 1960's, it was assassination—particularly, that of President John F. Kennedy. As McCarthy had savaged the Department of State for its supposed hospitality to communists, so Garrison vilified the Warren Commission for its verdict on America's most devastating crime. Garrison viewed the Shaw prosecution as a political platform, pure and simple. The real defendant was not Shaw, it was the Warren Report. When he told the jurors they sat "in judgment of Clay Shaw" he was telling them yet another untruth.

Clay Shaw was an unlikely excuse for a murder prosecution. He was a quiet, aesthetic looking man, with no criminal record of any kind. Garrison selected him for prosecution because he had had the misfortune of being named by one Perry Russo as a participant in a cocktail party conversation. Russo was a psychologically disturbed young insurance salesman from New Orleans who "thought" Shaw had been present when Lee Harvey Oswald and a man named David Ferrie discussed the prospective killing of the President. Ferrie, and, of course, Oswald, were conveniently dead by the time Shaw's case came to trial.

On cross-examination Russo admitted making some out of court statements that destroyed his already minuscule credibility. He had called the Shaw investigation "the most blown up and confused thing I have ever seen"; he had admitted he, "did not know the difference between fantasy and reality"; that he wished "he had never gotten involved in this mess"; that he did not think the conversation between Oswald, Ferrie and Shaw "sounded like a legitimate plot", but more like they were "shooting the breeze"; that the conversation was "vague" in his mind and he could not "truthfully say who said what"; and that he would like to have a chance to talk to Shaw and resolve his doubts about whether he was the same man he had heard talking with Ferrie and Oswald.

Garrison knew that Shaw had nothing to do with Kennedy's assassination, and the jury knew he knew. The final tipoff was that closing argument. It was not an argument at all, but a press release. It had been a long time since a lawyer had read a written argument to a jury, but Garrison unself-consciously did so. He did not even read it well—but that made no difference; his true audience was not in that New Orleans courtroom, but in the newspaper-reading, television-watching households of America.

After telling the jury that it sat "in judgment of Clay Shaw", Garrison never referred to the defendant again. He focused totally on ripping the Warren Report. With apparently unconscious irony, he said that "the government's handling of the investigation of President Kennedy's assassination was … the greatest fraud in the history of our Country, probably the greatest fraud in the history of mankind."

When Shaw was acquitted hardly anyone noticed. And why should they have? The prosecution was never about Clay Shaw, he was a pretext not a defendant, as artificial a part of the artificial proceedings as Garrison's canned speech. As McCarthy had used the Nation's fear, so Garrison used its profound sorrow, to build a slimy little pedestal for himself.

73.

AN HISTORIC LOW IN PSYCHIATRIC TESTIMONY

"I copied almost exactly ... I'm not the best writer in the world."

Dr. Martin M. Schorr, testifying in the prosecution of Sirhan Sirhan for the assassination of Robert F. Kennedy, 1969.

Dr. Schorr essentially volunteered to testify on behalf of Sirhan. He wrote a letter to Sirhan's defense counsel, saying that, based upon news accounts, Sirhan "sounded" schizophrenic. He closed by extending "wishes for a hopeful outcome".

Sirhan's lawyers accepted the implied invitation, and made Schorr their lead expert witness at the trial. His testimony went on at learned length, but the essence of it was a single sentence: "He [Sirhan] finds a symbolic replica of his father in the form of Kennedy, kills him and also removes the relationship that stands between him and his most precious possession—his mother's love."

On cross-examination, the prosecutor charged that Schorr's testimony was phony, being copied from a case report about the "Mad Bomber", who had terrorized New York City. When Schorr admitted the plagiarism, whatever value his testimony might have had went down the proverbial drain. In his final argument, defense counsel Grant Cooper contessed that he "could have crawled under the table" when Schorr made his humiliating admission.

The Schorr testimony gave a disreputable cast to all of the psychiatric testimony, which the prosecutors brutally exploited. Prosecutor Dan Compton quoted the Charles Dickens line, "the law is a ass, a idiot" ... "The law became an ass," he said, "the day it let psychiatrists get their hands on it ... I think it would be a frightening thing for the administration of criminal justice in this state if a case of this magnitude turns on whether [the defendant] saw clowns playing patty cake, or saw them kicking each other on the shins in his ink blot tests. I say, throw [the psychiatrists] all out in one big bag".

Compton's argument struck home, not only because of Schorr's dishonesty, but because it told a truth. Although a necessary component of any humane justice system, psychiatric testimony has been a canker sore in ours for generations. Insanity defenses, aided and abetted by "scientific" testimony, produce a troubling conjunction of realities: 1) everyone who murders or seriously attempts murder is, for that moment at least, abnormal; 2) a psychiatrist can always be found to convincingly convert that abnormality into mental incapacity; and 3) mental incapacity erases criminal responsibility. The state of mind that produces murder may prevent its punishment.

It has always been thought unjust to punish the truly mad. There was, in the beginning of the common law, the "Wild Beast test" of insanity, which was superseded by the "Counting Twenty Pence" test. In the 19th Century, the English developed the McNaughton Rule, which held that the defendant was legally insane if he did not know right from wrong, or did not understand the "nature and quality" of his criminal acts. 20th Century America invented the "irresistible impulse" defense, which prosecutors dealt with by asking: "Would the impulse have been irresistible if there had been a policeman watching?" Then came an ultra-liberal test, invented, curiously, by a judge from granite-ribbed New Hampshire. There is a defense of insanity, ruled Justice Doe, if the crime is, in any way, the product of a mental disease or condition.

Few jurisdictions adopted this shapeless concept, which if generally adopted, might have obliged America to release most of the serious criminals it held in confinement. But the similar 20th Century principle of "diminished criminal capacity" kept psychiatric witnesses well employed. If the defendant is just a little bit nuts, this concept said, he is a little less guilty and a little less subject to punishment. That is essentially what was going on in the Sirhan case—"Imprison him if you must, but don't give him death".

The jurors didn't buy it. They imposed the death penalty on the little Arab, with Schorr's testimony ringing in their ears. It was a sad day for the psychiatric profession, but a fairly good one for the administration of justice.[6]

---

6   The death sentence was later commuted to life imprisonment because of a 1972 Supreme Court decision that temporarily outlawed executions.

74.

THE MOST QUOTED JUDICIAL STATEMENT SINCE THE RETIREMENT OF OLIVER WENDELL HOLMES

"I can't define obscenity but I know it when I see it."

Justice Potter Stewart. (1972).

When Stewart said that he could judge obscenity only by viewing the particular publication or film at issue, he was stating a mundane truth. The justices actually made their decisions in obscenity cases by trooping into a film room and viewing the offending evidence. The only justices absent from the audiences were Black and Douglas, who believed that the First Amendment barred obscenity prosecutions under any circumstances. For the rest, the task was a daunting one. How could they decide in the abstract whether a movie "appealed predominantly to prurient interests, while lacking any redeeming social value"—the constitutional definition of obscenity. These generalized words hardly solved the problem of separating subtly artistic, barely acceptable, and outright abominable communications. And so the judges attended the movies, and decided their criminality based on visceral responses.

To a lesser extent, this is true of other areas of modern Supreme Court adjudication. The more the justices depart from interpreting the actual language of the Constitution, and derive vaguely expressed principles from them, the more personal their decisions become. Should abortions be allowed, and if so, to what extent and under what conditions? Should teenagers be subjected to the death penalty and, if so, at what age and for what crimes? Should lawyer advertising be protected by the First Amendment and, if so, under what circumstances and to what extent?

The justices cannot answer these questions by applying settled principles of law. What they mostly do is tell us that "we know a due process violation when [we] see one". And how could it be otherwise? The Constitution says nothing, directly or indirectly, about trimester abortions, executions of youths at any age, or legal advertisements as protected speech. The justices are, to put it bluntly, basically on their own in defining these Court-created issues. No wonder—as with the obscenity cases—they find it difficult to decide them until they "see them in the flesh". That is what gave Stewart's mundane statement its contemporary immortality. He was stating a simple truth that none of his colleagues, past, present or future, have been willing to state—applying basic constitutional principles has become an increasingly subjective process.

75.

THE WORD LOS ANGELES MUNICIPAL COURT DEFENSE LAWYERS MOST DREADED TO HEAR

"Forthwith."

Judge Noel Cannon, 1972-73.

Judge Cannon of the Los Angeles Municipal Court was a petty judicial tyrant, but by no means an ordinary one. She painted her chambers shocking pink, during court proceedings she kept a mechanical parrot by her side and a chihuahua puppy in her lap, and she once threatened to give an offending police officer "a 38 caliber vasectomy". Her favorite professional pastime was humiliating young defense lawyers and sending them to jail for imagined contempts of court.

It happened to Deputy Public Defender Todd Ridgeway on November 30, 1972, when he was in Judge Cannon's court defending a burglary charge. His cross-examination of a prosecution witness swiftly ended in disaster.

Ridgeway:	(I will call off the credit cards and try to …
The Court:	(You will not name off the credit cards. Please proceed with another question.
Ridgeway:	(Was it a Sands' credit card?
The Court:	(Perhaps you didn't hear the Court's ruling, Mr. Ridgeway.
Ridgeway:	(I think …
The Court:	(Answer the question. Did you or did you not hear the Court's ruling?
Ridgeway:	(Yes, Your Honor. I heard the ruling. I think …

The Court:	(Then you are asking—are you asking for what I think you are asking for? I've gone through this yesterday. You have had your last chance. Today is the day and I think now is the time. Are you ready?
Ridgeway:	(I don't understand, Your Honor.
The Court:	(Take Mr. Ridgeway into custody, <u>forthwith</u>. Get another public defender.

The fate of Deputy Public Defender John L. Ryan was even more bizarre. At 10:15 a.m. on April 6, 1973, he was assigned to represent the defendant in a preliminary hearing on 11 rape and kidnaping charges. At 11:02 he informed Judge Cannon that he needed additional time to prepare the case, and left the courtroom. The judge called the case for hearing at 11:36 and when it appeared that Ryan was not present, she issued a bench warrant for his arrest, setting bail at $25,000. When Ryan reappeared in court, the following proceedings ensued:

The Court:	(Alright now, I have had enough of this nonsense, Mr. Ryan.
Ryan:	(What nonsense, Your Honor?
The Court:	(Mr. Ryan, as it happens, I am not your witness and you are not cross-examining the Court. I have not yet heard an apology for your abominable behavior.
Ryan:	(I would apologize if I knew what that behavior was, Your Honor.
The Court:	(Alright. You are held in contempt of court. Found in direct contempt of this Court in the immediate view and presence of the Court and you are ordered into custody, <u>forthwith</u>. Bail is set at $25,000.
Ryan:	(Thank you, Your Honor.
The Court: Y	(ou're welcome.

Deputy Public Defender Michael Karozian suffered a similar fate on May 3, 1973, during a routine cross-examination of the prosecuting witness in a bad check case. Karozian cut the witness off in the middle of an answer, as lawyers will tend to do.

The Court:	(Let him finish. Now, Mr. Karozian, I don't want you continually interrupting the witness.
Karozian:	(That answer isn't responsive to my question, Your Honor.
The Court:	(Mr. Karozian, as I told you yesterday, as I have told you for the last time, that is for the Court to determine and not for you to determine. Do you understand that?
Karozian:	(Yes, Your Honor.

* * * *

	(May I continue, Your Honor?
The Court:	(You may. (At this point, Karozian apparently indulged in some sort of gesture or facial expression).
	(Alright, Mr. Karozian. Did you bring your toothbrush? Are you ready to suffer the consequences for being contemptuous to the Court, because that's what you are being.
Karozian:	(Well, Your Honor, at this point I would like to say I am trying to give the best defense possible that I can to my client.
The Court:	(Mr. Karozian, why don't you try opening your ears and closing your mouth for a bit? I warned you and you take no heed.
	(Please rise.
Karozian:	(Yes, Your Honor
The Court:	(Put your hands down to your side.
Karozian:	(Your Honor, at this time, I would like to inform the Court that I am not a child and that my demeanor ...
The Court:	(Alright. You are held in contempt. (<u>Forthwith</u>, Mr. Bailiff. <u>Forthwith</u>. (With you bring Mr. Kascoutasn in please? Take care of Mr. Karozian, <u>forthwith</u>.

On July 12, 1975, the Supreme Court of California finally caught up with Judge Cannon, throwing her out of office after 12 years on the Bench. The Court's opinion cited 21 acts of "willful judicial misconduct" and eight acts which "brought her judicial office into disrepute". It concluded that:

> [Judge Cannon] has engaged in a course of conduct which has maligned her judicial office and clearly establishes her lack of temperament and ability to perform judicial functions in an even-handed manner. Because it is our duty to preserve the integrity and independence of the judiciary, we order Judge Noel Cannon of the Municipal Court for the Los Angeles Judicial District of Los Angeles County removed from office. The order is final <u>forthwith</u>.

"Forthwith," Judge Cannon, forthwith.

76.

THE QUIET BEGINNING OF THE DESTRUCTION OF A PRESIDENCY

"I'm even worried ... that I'm getting too big for my britches."

Watergate Special Prosecutor Archibald Cox. (October 20, 1973).

During the Watergate investigation Special Prosecutor Archibald Cox subpoenaed numerous tapes of conversations held in the President's office, at least one of which Nixon knew was starkly incriminating. He and his "people" immediately went to work devising a "modified compliance" with the subpoena.

At 8:18 p.m., EST on Friday, October 19, 1973, Press Secretary Ron Ziegler issued an announcement, stating that a "compromise" had been reached on the production of the tapes. (It was unclear who the parties to the compromise were, since Cox had not been consulted.) The White House would prepare summaries of the tapes, the announcement stated, which would be verified by the venerable and ill Southern Democratic Senator John Stennis. The summaries would be turned over to the Court *in lieu* of the tapes, and there would be no further subpoenas of tapes or personal presidential papers by the Special Prosecutor.

Cox knew that he had to beat the White House to the punch in the public relations fight. He had to explain that there was no compromise as far as he was concerned; that the Stennis plan would "deprive prosecutors of admissible evidence"; and that it would be up to the Court to decide whether to accept Nixon's proposal. Cox scheduled a press conference for Saturday morning to explain why he could not accept the "compromise". He was terrified at the prospect of disobeying a presidential order, particularly since Senator Ervin, the hero of the legislative hearings during the previous summer, had endorsed the Stennis plan. According to Cox's wife "Archie was beside himself for fear that he would bring down the Republic".

The press conference was held at the National Press Club before an overflowing crowd. Cox began by nervously saying "I am certainly not out to get the President of the United States. I'm even worried ... that I'm getting too big for my britches, that what I see as principle could be vanity. I hope not." But, he said, he simply could not accept Nixon's "deal", given his assigned duty to fully and fairly investigate the allegations against the Administration.

The infamous Saturday Night Massacre ensued. The White House instructed Attorney General Richardson to fire Cox. Richardson resigned. Deputy Attorney General William Ruckelshaus was then told to carry out the order and when he refused to do so he was fired. After much hand-wringing and pacing the floor Robert Bork, who was next in line at the Department of Justice, carried out the order and Cox was gone.

In retrospect the "massacre" made Nixon's eventual resignation inevitable. There were many things about the Watergate scandal the public didn't understand, and the people had a natural resistance to removing any president from office. But firing the quiet, dignified, fair-minded Cox because he refused to violate his oath of office was understood by everyone, and was shocking to almost everyone. A growing conviction spread among the people and Congress that Nixon simply wasn't worth keeping. The Supreme Court eventually forced Nixon to give up the incriminating tape in response to a subpoena issued by Cox's successor, Leon Jaworski. Traveling with unstoppable momentum, what began on the morning of October 20, 1973 came to an inevitable conclusion in August, 1974 when the President resigned his office.

77.

AN HISTORIC DOUBLE ENTENDRE

"When we impose [the death penalty] we know not what we do."

Anthony Amsterdam in *Greg v. Georgia* (1976).

Professor Amsterdam was making a philosophical/religious point: since we don't know what death is we have no moral right to impose it as a criminal punishment. As the years went by, however, his argument took on a distressing second meaning. DNA testing and other scrupulous investigations eventually revealed that scores of innocent inmates had entered death rows after the Professor had lost his argument, and capital punishment was retained. In the most horrifically practical sense, those inmates were there because, in each of their cases, the authorities didn't know what they were doing.

Obviously, Amsterdam knew when he spoke that the death penalty was flawed in its application, and he stressed that point in his argument. But had he been able to demonstrate "we know not what we do" by telling the justices that innocent human beings were regularly being sent to death row, think of the added power his argument would have had, and the decision it might have produced. If scores of innocents were sentenced to death in the decades that followed his argument, think of the countless innocent people who had been judicially murdered in the centuries that preceded it. If we had known more about "what we were doing", and what we had done, when the *Greg* case was argued, America might have conceivably joined the rest of the civilized world in doing away with capital punishment.

78.

A CRUEL AND UNUSUAL DECISION

"We ... hold that the mandatory life sentence imposed upon this petitioner does not constitute cruel and unusual punishment under the Eighth and Fourteenth Amendments."

U.S. Supreme Court affirming the life sentence of Scotty Rummel for having failed to fix an air-conditioner after being paid $120.75 to do so. 1980.

Technically, Scotty Rummel had lived a life of crime. In the seriousness of his criminal endeavors, however, he was no Al Capone.

In 1964, at the age of 22, he used a credit card an acquaintance had given him to charge $80.00 worth of tires at a service station in San Antonio, Texas. He admitted to police that he "sorta" knew that his friend had stolen the card. He pleaded guilty and received a three year prison sentence, of which he served 20 months.

In 1969, at the age of 27, he paid his weekly motel rental charge of $28.36 with a forged check. He pleaded guilty and was sentenced to four years in prison, of which he served 18 months.

In 1972, at the age of 30, he offered to repair an air-conditioner in a San Antonio bar. The owner gave him a check for $120.75 to purchase a compressor. The supply company wouldn't sell the compressor to him because he wasn't an authorized dealer, so he cashed the check at a local bank, signing his name and the name of the supply company. He never got around to buying a compressor or repairing the air-conditioner, and was finally arrested for stealing the $120.75 from the bar owner. This time he went to trial. His court-appointed lawyer called no witnesses and advised Rummel not to testify. Rummel's parents had paid the bar owner $50.00 on account and he had signed a non-prosecution agreement, but the trial judge refused to allow it into evidence. The only testimony the jury heard was that Rummel had cashed the check and was not an employee of the bar. Having been presented with no reasonable alternative, the jury returned a conviction.

Unfortunately for Rummel, Texas had a law requiring that a life sentence be imposed on anyone convicted of three felonies. Although Rummel's three offenses had netted him a grand total of $229.11, he qualified for life imprisonment, which was duly imposed. His case eventually made it to the United States Supreme Court, where his lawyer argued that his sentence constituted "cruel, unusual and excessive" punishment under the Eighth Amendment to the United States Constitution.

Rummel's punishment certainly seemed to fit the bill. He had been sentenced to spend the rest of his days in jail for conduct that was marginally criminal, to the extent it was criminal at all. But the Supreme Court wouldn't buy his argument. It used 44 pages of solemn legalese to decide, by a five to four vote, that a life sentence for stealing $229.11 was good justice in the Land of the Free. Justice Powell's dissenting opinion was incredulous. "We are construing a living Constitution," he protested. "The sentence imposed upon the petitioner would be viewed as grossly unjust by virtually every layman and lawyer." That was probably true—it had taken the careful winnowing of the Supreme Court selection process to find five individuals who thought otherwise.

The "philosophy" of the *Rummel* decision would have been a hideous blot on Supreme Court jurisprudence had it been allowed to stand, but three years later the Court returned to clean up the mess. Jerry Helm had been given a life sentence by a South Dakota court for committing seven minor offenses. This time the Supreme Court held, by an identical five to four vote, that the sentence was unconstitutional. The flip-flop was produced by Justice Harry Blackmun, whose definition of "cruel, inhuman and excessive" had apparently changed between 1980 and 1983.

It was Chief Justice Warren Burger's turn to be incredulous. The Court's rapid switch in position was unforgivable, his dissenting opinion said. It represented a government of "men" instead of "law". More precisely, it represented the government of one man—Justice Blackmun—and thank God for him.

79.

THE STRANGEST RIGHT OF PRIVACY DECISION OF ALL TIME

> "[Although it was really a 'reception' in football parlance] the recording is an 'interception' as our Supreme Court has construed that term, and may not be offered into evidence."
>
> Florida Court of Appeals, 1984.

On March 14, 1984, an accused killer was set free, when a Florida appeals court ruled that his victim had illegally recorded his own murder. Anthony Paul Inciarrano was charged with killing Eavin Herman Trimble, a psychiatrist and marriage counselor. The crime was alleged to have taken place in Dr. Trimble's office, during a hostile meeting on the evening of July 6, 1982.

The sole evidence against Inciarrano consisted of a tape recording surreptitiously made by Trimble at the time of the fatal interview. The tape produced a sensation when it was played during a hearing in the trial court. It began with an angry conversation between Trimble and a voice identifiable as Inciarrano's, concerning a business deal that had "gone sour". There was a clicking sound, followed by five apparent gun shots and what sounded, in the words of the court, like "the gushing of blood". The tape ended with the sound of retreating footsteps and silence.

Inciarrano entered a plea of *nolo contendere*, or no contest, and filed a motion to suppress the tape, on the ground that the recording violated Florida privacy law. He cited a statute that prohibited the "interception" by electronic means of "any oral conversation".

Inciarrano's attorney contended that the recording of the death scene was an "interception" of Inciarrano's conversation with Trimble, which violated his client's "legitimate expectation of privacy". Since the recording was illegal, the lawyer argued, it could not be used as evidence against the defendant.

The trial court rejected the motion, ruling that, while it is understandable that killers should desire that their conduct be kept secret, they are not entitled to the law's assistance in doing so. The judge stated that Inciarrano's expectation of privacy had "dissolved in the sound of gunfire".

Showing no appetite for the necessity of doing so, the Florida Court of Appeals reversed the trial court's decision and effectively set the defendant free. The judges did not personally believe that the recording was an "interception" within the meaning of the statute, but felt bound by previous rulings of the Florida Supreme Court that indicated it was. The Court stated its own view by means of a football analogy, which labeled Trimble's recording a "reception" rather than an "interception":

> A reasonable layman familiar with the game of football might well comment that if a pass from the quarterback to the tight end of the team on offense was scored as an interception, the quarterback might be more than a little chagrined. It would be assumed that such a play is more properly scored a reception.... [I]n common parlance, the term 'interception' implies a stopping by someone other than the intended receiver.

Since the defendant's words and bullets were directed toward the victim, the Court believed that he should be treated as a receiver rather than an interceptor. The judges nonetheless felt compelled to bow to the reasoning of the less sports-wise Supreme Court, whose decisions seemed to compel the opposite result.

In *Olmstead v. United States*, (1928), Justice Brandeis had disapproved the judicial use of evidence obtained by police wire-tapping, on the ground that it encouraged illegal conduct. "The law is the great, the omnipresent teacher," he wrote, "it teaches the whole people by its example." Presumably, the Court of Appeals' teaching in the Inciarrano case was that private recording of consensual telephone conversations is wrong, and should be discouraged. If so, Dr. Trimble certainly learned his lesson.[7]

---

7   The Florida Supreme Court later came to its senses, and reversed the Court of Appeals ruling. Presumably, Inciarrano ultimately got what he deserved.

80.

DRUNKEN JUSTICE

"Guildy as charg'd."

Florida District Court, 1986.

No recording of it exists, but the verdict in *State v. Conver and Tanner* must have had a slurred sound when it was announced. It was returned in a federal prosecution involving complex charges of fraud, relating to a one and a half billion dollar loan transaction.

After the verdict was returned, two of the jurors contacted the defense lawyers and gave them some appalling information. They said that, from the jury's perspective, the trial had been "one big party". During lunches and at recesses, jurors had consumed large quantities of alcohol and drugs. The foreperson was "an alcoholic" who polished off a liter of wine a day, other jurors regularly consumed a pitcher of beer a piece at lunch. Some jurors routinely used marijuana and cocaine, separately and in combination with each other, and with various kinds of alcohol. As a result, "jurors were falling asleep all the time during the trial" and did not seem to know what was going on. One of the informants said that the heaviest cocaine user admitted during a recess that he was "flying". The informant admitted that his own level of intoxication made it difficult for him to follow the evidence.

These statements were put into sworn affidavits and submitted to the court, in support of a motion which insisted that the jury had not been sober and awake enough to understand the case. The court denied the motion.

On appeal before the U.S. Supreme Court, the defendants argued that the affidavits demonstrated that they had been convicted by an incompetent jury, and that at the very least, further inquiry should be made. By a five-four vote, the Court rejected the argument, citing the importance of "protecting jury deliberations from intrusive inquiry." There might be evidence that the verdict had been produced by a jury too drunk and high to know what it was doing, but the verdict could not be "impeached," and the convictions must stand. The jury's deliberations must remain a mystery, albeit a farcical one.

This ruling was an echo from the distant past. When juries first appeared on the scene in the 13th Century they were, as English historian James Stephen wrote, a "newer sort of ordeal. The Court accepted [the verdict] unquestioningly, as it used to accept the pronouncements of the hot iron or the cold water.... The jury was no more regarded as 'rational' than the ordeals which it replaced, and just as one did not question the judgments of God as shown in the ordeal, so the verdict of the jury was equally inscrutable."

Over the centuries, the jury became a fact-finder that was supposed to arrive at truth through a logical reasoning process, but courts stubbornly clung to the notion that jury deliberations must remain "inscrutable" expressions of the people's will. Which is why, eight decades into the 20th Century, Mr. Conver and Mr. Tanner could be sent to prison by a drugged and drunken jury, with the approval of our highest Court.

81.

DEFENDING SOCIETY AGAINST CONFESSIONS

"There is no evidence more unreliable than a confession."

John Mortimer, in "Rumpole on Trial", (1992).

Rumpole had good reason to make this statement. He had just been through a trial featuring a confession that had been deliberately altered by the police. On the personal side, his former partner Guthrie Featherstone had all but ruined his marriage by falsely boasting to his comrades that he had had an affair with a legal secretary. Crooked law enforcement. Weak male ego. It was enough to make anyone mistrust confessions.

But Rumpole was expressing a general point of view peculiar to English and American lawyers. Our common legal tradition strives to be fair in ways that baffle the rest of the world, and the most prominent of these ways is our prejudice against confessions.

Of all the Supreme Court criminal law rulings that troubled America in the 1960's, the most troubling were those dealing with confessions. In *Miranda v. Arizona*, the Supreme Court held that a suspect could not be questioned until he was advised of his right to remain silent, his right to have appointed counsel present, and the fact that his statements could be used against him in court. The average American thought this ruling was perverse—if the authorities wanted to obtain a confession, they first had to make every effort <u>to convince the suspect not to confess</u>! The American legal system inherited its prejudice against confessions from the Mother Country. It is an attitude deeply rooted in English national pride. Centuries ago when the jury system was coming into its own, England's bitter political enemy, France, was developing a criminal justice system based upon torture. The French theory was that confessions were the most reliable form of evidence, even when induced by physical pain. The English believed that this was a barbaric point of view. They touted their jury system as a humane truth finder, which expressed the noble English character, in counter-distinction to the use of coerced confessions, which expressed the depraved character of the French.

Eschewing confessional justice became obsessive. 19th Century English court rulings on the admissibility of confessions make the American *Miranda* decisions look like a revival of the Spanish Inquisition. Displaying what has been called "irrational sentimentality" toward confessed criminals, the courts consistently ruled that almost any inducement or threat rendered confessions useless as evidence. A confession was excluded in one case because the suspect was offered a glass of gin during interrogation; in another, because a poster offering a small reward for evidence was tacked on the wall of the office in which the suspect was questioned; in another, because the defendant was told that what he said would be used "against" him. Hostility toward confessions became so pervasive that police officers began to believe that they were illegal *per se*. One English constable, when asked whether the defendant had made a statement, replied: "No; he was beginning to do so, but I know my duty better, and I prevented him."

English courts have gotten a bit tougher in the 20th Century—colorful though his career was, Rumpole never encountered anything like the above. There nonetheless persists a sense, in both England and America, that government prosecutions should essentially be run as "do it yourself" enterprises. It is a healthy, if unusual, prejudice.

82.

THE LAW BECOMES SENILE IN ITS OLD AGE

"The Bennis automobile ... facilitated and was used in criminal activity. Both the trial court and the Michigan Supreme Court followed our long-standing practice, and the judgment of the Supreme Court of Michigan is therefore affirmed."

The United States Supreme Court, approving the confiscation of an automobile owned by Mrs. Bennis, because her husband had sex in it with a prostitute. *State v. Bennis*, 1996.

The "practice" which the bizarre *Bennis* ruling invoked was, indeed, a "long-standing" one. The idea that objects used in committing crimes can be forfeited and taken from their owners, even though the owners are innocent of any wrongdoing, goes back to the dim beginnings of English law. Taking a woman's automobile from her because her husband had committed adultery in it with a prostitute is puzzling to contemporary Americans, but it would have been well understood by the inhabitants of Dark Ages England.

From the beginnings of Anglo-Saxon law until the 14th Century, English courts "convicted" boats, carts, swords and trees that caused injury or death, and "sentenced" them to be destroyed. These so-called "deodands" or "banes" were thought of, in a real sense, as criminals. "If you hand your sword over to a smith", wrote legal historian F. W. Maitland, "see that you get it back 'sound'; that is to say, with no blood-guiltiness attached to it, for otherwise you may be receiving a 'bane' into your house ... [M]any boats bore the guilt that should have been ascribed to beer".

The legally-mandated destruction of deodands was a matter of vengeance. They had committed crimes and must pay the price. "[T]he claim of the soul hurried out of this world outweighed the claim of the dead man's kinfolk. They will have received the bane, not as compensation for the loss they suffered, but rather as an object upon which their vengeance must be wrecked, before the dead man may lie in peace."

The idea that the property of an innocent owner could be forfeited was always an accepted part of American law. An 1819 opinion by Chief Justice Marshall, approving the forfeiture of a damage-causing sea vessel, reads like the decree of a Saxon judge prescribing the destruction of a murderous tree limb. "This is not a proceeding against the owner" Marshall explained, "It is a proceeding against the vessel for an offense by the vessel." In a similar case, Justice Joseph Story stated that: "The thing here is primarily considered as the offender, or rather the offense is primarily attached to the thing."

Commenting on these holdings, Oliver Wendell Holmes pronounced them inane: "These great judges, although of course aware that a ship is no more alive than a mill wheel, thought that not only did the law in fact deal with it as if it were alive, but that it was reasonable that the law should do so."

As Mrs. Bennis discovered, the inanity of the concept did not make it any less "the law". There was, however, a bright side to her situation—she was lucky that her husband didn't bring the prostitute home with him. The government would probably have foreclosed on her house.

83.

CAPITAL PUNISHMENT TURNS WACKY

> "In our view, rape ... does not ordinarily constitute ... serious physical abuse within the meaning of the statute ... and we must reject the conclusion that the three stab wounds evidenced in this case constituted ... serious physical injury beyond that necessary to produce death."
>
> Tennessee Supreme Court, 1996.

As murder cases go, the facts in *State v. Odom* were about as ugly as it gets. A gentle, 78-year-old virgin named Mina Ethel Johnson was stabbed, raped, and then stabbed repeatedly again until she was dead in the back seat of her car in Memphis, Tennessee. The murderer, Richard Odom, had robbed and murdered another woman 13 years earlier. He had been convicted and sentenced to life without parol, but had escaped from the penitentiary about a month before he met Ms. Odom on May 10, 1991.

He had intended only to steal her purse, he explained, but there was no money in it. She offered to write him a check and give him her diamond ring, but he pulled her into the back seat instead, and cut her with a knife. "Don't do this, son," she had begged, and that seemed to enrage him. "I'll give you a son," he muttered savagely, and that is when he raped her.

"After that [the rape] I just wanted to kill her," Odom said; so he stabbed her in the heart, in the lungs and in the liver, in the process lacerating her hands which she had raised in self defense; and left the frail corpse alone in the night, draining blood.

He was arrested, convicted and sentenced to death by a Memphis jury. But on appeal, in June of 1996, the Tennessee Supreme Court reversed the judgment and sent the case back for re-sentencing. There was insufficient proof of "aggravating circumstances" to justify putting Odom to death under Tennessee's capital punishment law, the Court explained.

The Court's opinion bristled with semantics, but what it came down to was this: the murder was not bad enough to qualify for capital punishment.

In reaching this astounding conclusion, the justices engaged in a sort of Jack the Ripper contest. They set out to determine whether Odom, demonstrably a cruel, brutal, cold-blooded murderer, was among "the worst of the worst"— for only in that case could he qualify for death. The justices did not specify what sort of murderer they had in mind—indeed, it seemed doubtful that Jack himself would have passed muster—but they were meticulous in stating why Odom failed to measure up.

Under the Tennessee statute, which had been enacted to conform to U.S. Supreme Court rulings, a murderer could be sentenced to death only if he committed his crime "in an especially heinous, atrocious, cruel, or an exceptionally depraved manner ... which must involve torture, or serious physical abuse, beyond that necessary to produce death." Surely Odom's crime met these lurid adjectival and physical requirements. Not so, said the Court's opinion. Mina Ethel Johnson's murder may have been heinous, atrocious, cruel and depraved, but there was not the requisite "torture" or "serious physical abuse beyond that necessary to produce death".

Well, what about the rape, the prosecutors asked. Not bad enough, the Court replied. "In our view, rape ... does not ordinarily constitute 'torture' or 'serious physical abuse' within the meaning of the statute." Besides, if <u>rape</u> qualified a murderer for capital punishment, the death penalty would be more common than the law allows. Death must be confined to a worse class of predators than those who merely rape and murder.

Well, then, what about all those stab wounds in the lady's arms, hands, heart, lungs and liver? The Court's response was opaquely magisterial: "[W]e must reject the conclusion that the three stab wounds (which three?) evidenced in this case constituted 'torture' or 'serious physical injury beyond that necessary to produce death'", it said—and let it go at that. The Court seemed to be saying that Odom wasn't an especially atrocious murderer, just an especially inefficient one.

Most of Tennessee thought that the *Odom* opinion was, itself, "atrocious", and some even suggested that it was "depraved". It cost one of the justices her seat on the Court in a popular referendum two months later.

But the Tennessee Supreme Court should not shoulder all of the blame for *State v. Odom*. That decision, and many others like it across the nation, bring to mind an old baseball story. Exasperated by the sloppy play of his right fielder during practice, the manager trots out to show him how it is done. After muffing the first two fly balls hit to him and throwing the third ball into the stands, he slams his glove down and returns to the dugout. "Johnson," he barks, "you have right field so screwed up, <u>nobody</u> can play it."

The Tennessee justices who were maligned for their performance in the *Odom* case might well have directed a similar complaint at the U. S. Supreme Court. For—whatever one's views on capital punishment law—it could fairly be said that, by 1996, the Supreme Court had it so thoroughly "screwed up", nobody could apply it.

84.

THE SUPREME COURT'S SECOND WORST DECISION

"Although we may never know with complete certainty the identity of the winner of this year's Presidential election, the identity of the loser is perfectly clear. It is the Nation's confidence in the judge as an impartial guardian of the rule of law."

Justice John Paul Stevens, dissenting in *Bush v. Gore* (2000).

Justice Stevens was genuinely angry and deeply worried. He thought that his Court had rendered a decision that was immensely important, deeply flawed, and exuded the odor of personal political bias. A Republican himself, he believed in the marrow of his judicial soul, that his Republican brethren had violated the public trust in order to effectively appoint a Republican, George Bush, President of the United States.

The decision had every ingredient of the worst kind of judicial decision-making: it was bad law, its reasoning ran precisely contrary to the philosophies of the Justices who applied it, and it seemed to consciously serve the personal and political purposes of its five authors more purely than any Supreme Court decision in memory. If it was not a deliberate judicial hatchet job it might as well have been, considering its reasoning and effect. Any survey of Supreme Court decisions of the past two hundred years would have to rank it among the worst of the worst, only slightly less infamous than *Scott v. Sandford* (1856) which held that freed slaves could never become U.S. citizens.

The case is well known but imperfectly understood by most informed Americans. It was technical in its facts and reasoning however explosive in its results. It was the climax—really the anti-climax—of weeks of ballot counting and scrutiny followed by several Florida state court decisions. The Supreme Court's decision was a resounding negative that set all of this to rest. The recounting of the ballots must stop, preserving Bush's razor thin "victory". The volatile world of the Florida primary ended with a whimper, not a bang.

The author of the majority opinion was not identified. It was an anonymous *per curiam* opinion that was collectively agreed to by five Justices, none of whom took individual "credit" for it. The phantom author made it clear that the decision itself was a legal phantom. Ordinarily Supreme Court decisions not only resolve the disputes before them, but in doing so they make law. Later cases apply the principles they state in resolving their own disputes, and so it goes on and on through time. The technique is called *stare decisis* and the process is called the development of law.

Presumably not wishing to let the principles applied in *Bush v. Gore* survive to haunt their future, the anonymous five strangled those principles at birth. "Our consideration is limited to the present circumstance", the majority opinion warned, "for the problem of equal protection in election processes generally presents many complexities". In other words, this decision is legal authority for nothing beyond the boundaries of the case. Don't bother citing it in the future if the shoe should happen to be on the other political foot. It is not about election law, it's about George Bush, Albert Gore and the five of us. Apply the result, but conveniently forget how we got to it.

The Phantom Five got to their result, to put it bluntly, by pure intellectual dishonesty. Under Florida law the recount of disputed ballots required election officials to examine each ballot to determine the voter's "clear intent". If a ballot had been merely indented instead of being completely punched through, for example, or if a "chad" had been left hanging to the ballot instead of being completely ripped away, the question was whether a tentative voter had changed his mind at the last minute or had merely been careless in operating the apparatus.

In ordering a halt to the recount process the Phantom Five, who were ironically the most conservative of the Justices, acted in drastic, dramatic opposition to judicial conservative gospel. All things being equal, it might be thought they would refrain from any review of the Florida recount process. The U.S. Constitution provided that Presidential electors were to be appointed by whatever processes the states decreed. The very act of reviewing Florida's standard for ballot recounting, therefore, violated the usual state's rights credo of Conservatives. Here was the nasty federal government telling a state how to conduct its electoral process, and, amazingly, it was the Conservatives who were doing it.

The basis of the Court's decision to halt the recount was even more astounding. Ever since *Brown v. Board* of Education, "equal protection" had been a major decisional tool for liberal Justices. It was a very useful tool because few, if any, aspects of human conduct are literally equal. As John Kennedy famously said "life is unfair".

In the past, the Phantom Five had been notably willing to tolerate life's natural unfairness. Justice Thomas, for example, had written in a 1996 dissenting opinion that "[t]he Equal Protection Clause shields only against purposeful discrimination". (Emphasis added). The colleagues who joined him in the majority opinion in *Bush v. Gore* were to varying degrees similarly inclined. Certainly none of them ordinarily favored using the federal Equal Protection Clause to consign reasonable state processes to the dust bin.

But they did so in the *Bush v. Gore* decision. That decision's main point was that determining votes on the basis of the Florida standard of "clear intent" is so vague a process that its application by different people to different ballots violates the Equal Protection Clause. The American legal system necessarily and routinely functions by the ascertainment of various people's intent by other people. To provide an admittedly gross example, one man dies in a gas chamber and another goes free or receives a reduced sentence because different juries have come to different conclusions as to the defendants' respective intents in committing certain acts years before. Not by scanning uniform ballots, but by listening to testimony given by witnesses with faded memories, motives to lie and whatever other psychological burdens they carried to the witness box. Gross as this example may be, it makes a relevant point. Government does not, and cannot, guarantee equality of results. It can only do its best to provide a level playing field. Conscientious election officials carefully attempting to determine actual voter intent by scrutinizing punched ballot cards surely meet that human standard.

Moreover, thirty-three other states used identical "intent of the voter" standards in recounts. Why not invalidate all recounts in all of these states, as when the Supreme Court invalidated all of America's death penalty statutes in 1972 because they were similar to the statutes under review? (Because it wasn't practical of course).

The comments about this bizarre and troubling decision have been close to unanimous. It has been called, not only "bad constitutional law", but "lawless", "illegitimate", "unprincipled", "partisan", "fraudulent", "disingenuous", and "motivated by improper considerations".

These commentators assumed that the decision would live in judicial infamy along with *Dred Scott v. Sandford*, but it hasn't turned out that way. After an initial outburst, criticism of *Bush v. Gore* became muted, and then all but disappeared. Americans became focused on Bush's performance in office, not on how he got there. Why did this terrible decision escape its deserved place in the basement of judicial history?

First, perhaps, because it was technical. The Court's novel application of the Equal Protection Clause appalled scholars but was hardly understood by the average citizen. When the *Dred Scott* Court declared ex-slaves non-citizens, everyone got it. When the *Bush* Court held that different vote counters might have different perceptions of voter intent, many missed the point or said "well, maybe so".

Secondly, the Court's decision was negative in its effect. Rather than doing or inflicting anything, it stopped the recount, leaving the process where it had been. The passivity of the result may have softened its impact on the people's psyches.

Finally, and perhaps most importantly, the decision was political in its effect. Half of the Nation were too happy with the result to care how it was reached and if the other half complained they could be dismissed as sore losers.

For whatever reason, *Bush v. Gore* remains the quietest of the few true injustices our Supreme Court has purportrated. Quiet or not, it was a hell of a way to begin a new millennium.

978-0-595-47556-8
0-595-47556-6

Made in the USA
Lexington, KY
09 May 2013